Advance Praise

Startup entrepreneurs are often visionaries and dreamers. Champions of their own creations. Deeply in love with their offering. And blind to simple questions such as 'who and how' to sell their offering. Having been part of a startup in a pioneering space, there have been many eye- and mind-openers on what we could have done better and what we should not have done the way it was done. Solutions come in hindsight.

The Startup's Guide to Sales as the book is named reflects the simplicity and directness of approach. No jazzy stuff. Simple clear steps that even a layman can understand. Starting with likening the starting a startup to falling in love, so aptly, to ending with 'Go and prosper', the book does what it says somewhere in one of its pages. It is sincere, honest and presentable in its approach to its customer, the reader. It tells not only 'what is right' and 'what is wrong' but also cautions 'what can go wrong'. And all in simple question and answer format, but much beyond an FAQ. In fact, it is a DEQ—deeply experienced questions—and of course answers for each of them. Covering from 'whether you need a sales team' to 'how to build a sales organization' to 'performance monitoring', not to forget the costs, margins and profits, the book is a primer, refresher, guide and reference for all entrepreneurs.

Just the right recipe for a love-blinded startup entrepreneur.

G. Srinivasan, *Co-founder, RuralShores Business Services,*
The World's Largest Rural BPO

The Startup's Guide to Sales explains lucidly the various aspects that a startup entrepreneur needs to consider for selling their product/ service to the target groups. The book doesn't use 'jargons' which makes it easy for the uninitiated to grasp the idea presented. The choice of channels, the importance of training in sales, the need for reports and their review and lastly but not least, the critical role that the entrepreneur must play as a leader of the sales team. The attention drawn towards the pitfalls is also very useful. The concepts of trade profitability as a means to convince the channel is explained in easily understandable steps. The best part is that the book would be useful even for sales and other professionals in established businesses and not necessarily startups!

Gautam Basu, *Management Consultant and PE Fund Advisor*

When we started, we were quite confident of one function, as co-founders all of us had started our careers in sales. But, In Paper Boat journey, we have made the maximum mistakes in sales, so I think the subject is relevant.

Ram was heading sales, when I joined Eveready as a noob in 1998. I was reminded of his teachings after reading this book. It was simply explained then with anecdotes and stories, and it is the same in this book. It was invaluable at that stage of my journey, and it remains invaluable.

June 1999, I was working with Roshan, then head of Eveready, in the Indore market and one of the products was dusty. He told me dust on product was the worst feeling for a salesperson and I immediately cleaned it with my hanky. Also, on that day, I was told to never wear lace shoes, as slip-ons were easy to remove when we entered an outlet. This book is full of such practical learning.

Neeraj Kakkar, *Co-founder of one of India's most loved brands, Paper Boat*

Once in a while, something comes to us that makes us want to sit up and take notice. Notice the fact that what one is holding in his/her hands is not ordinary. This is exactly the feeling I had when I went through this amazing experience of reading Roshan and Ram's book.

This is a tale of axioms and real-time experiences woven so perfectly into every detail, I would think this is not just a book or guide but almost the first bible on sales that I have come across. And resonated with my many years at various organizations and made me wonder how beautiful life would have been if I had something like this carved out for me in those days.

Roshan and Ram have managed to put in all that flashes through one's mind, especially when one has embarked on a startup. All the questions, the apprehensions and also the common doubts as to the relevance of GTM in a tech-obsessed society. Broken the walls between offline and online, distributor vs. direct, and all the cheap and weak vs. expensive and classy strategies.

The section on manpower is so crucial that an ingredient in today's world has been beautifully dissected on all the elements and I feel this alone can adorn the glass walls of corporates.

Overall, it's a must read and practice for every startup and also for many other established businesses where they may take a lesson or two from this masterpiece.

Vijay Parthasarathy, *Founder Advisor Indus OS,*
Brand specialist, Mind Coach, Speaker

In this book, strategy has been blended with simple tools in a user-friendly way that helps reduce complexity. Simplicity is at the core of this book.

The mental make-up needed for a startup is quite different from what is required in more mature organizations. Your competitors always seem to be chasing the same opportunities you chase.

Roshan and Ram highlight the importance and effectiveness of the 80/20 process that helps focus and redirect 'scarce' resources especially in a startup mode. I liked the practical 'how to do it' style adopted by the authors while highlighting the pros and cons of various sales models. A must read for startup entrepreneurs!

Ravi Gopalan, *Group Director, Human Resources, Illinois Tool Works Inc. (ITW), Illinois, USA*

Ram Menon, my sales guru, and Roshan Joseph, my mentor in marketing and team building, have come together to simplify the complex world of sales. I will always remember these words from them: 'Focus consumer! Always!! Either convince me, or get convinced! Trust people, everyone is out to do their best! Achieve business goals profitably, always work in a process-oriented manner. It is important to tell people BOTH … what should be done to what should not be done! Do the RIGHT things…, do things RIGHT. A treat for both startups and for those who have started and who are padding up to RUN.

Anil Bajaj, *Senior VP, Sales and Marketing, Eveready Industries*

This book is a boon for all who are thinking of a startup. Roshan Joseph has been a part of setting a sales team for our Saviesa, a startup in Home Improvement. We started less than two years ago and are happy to see the milestones reached. The book is written in language that is easy to understand and invaluable for the student of sales.

Rajesh T. Ahuja, *MD, Saviesa*

The challenges of selling a new product are enormous. This book provides the reader with a practical step-by-step understanding of how to go about it. Extremely useful for the *techpreneur* and a great refresher for the experienced.

Bijou Kurien, *Former President and CEO, Reliance Retail*

Roshan's second book is a bible for startups, especially if you are a technocrat founder who is now suddenly thrust into managing a team and extracting performance. Don't just read it as a guide to hiring/planning/building/training a sales team. Any founder/promoter would relate to most of the knowledge. The cross-functional applicability of these learnings is enormous.

Dr Harsha Guduru, *Founder, Cureosity Healthcare*

The
STARTUP'S
GUIDE to
SALES

The STARTUP'S GUIDE to SALES

How Not to Crash and Burn

Roshan Louis Joseph
Ram Mohan Menon

SAGE | Response Business Books

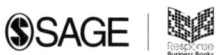

Los Angeles | London | New Delhi
Singapore | Washington DC | Melbourne

First published in 2020 by

SAGE Publications India Pvt Ltd
B1/I-1 Mohan Cooperative Industrial Area
Mathura Road, New Delhi 110 044, India
www.sagepub.in

SAGE Publications Inc
2455 Teller Road
Thousand Oaks, California 91320, USA

SAGE Publications Ltd
1 Oliver's Yard, 55 City Road
London EC1Y 1SP, United Kingdom

SAGE Publications Asia-Pacific Pte Ltd
18 Cross Street #10-10/11/12
China Square Central
Singapore 048423

Published by Vivek Mehra for SAGE Publications India Pvt Ltd. Typeset in 12/15 pts Perpetua by Fidus Design Pvt Ltd, Chandigarh.

Library of Congress Control Number: 2019953107

ISBN: 978-93-5328-936-2 (PB)

SAGE Team: Manisha Mathews and Shruti Gupta
Illustrations credit: Ajoy Joseph

To Karen and Michelle, daughters from heaven, who made
Amrish and Ajoy lucky sons, and our family blessed.

—Roshan Joseph

To my dear wife Daya, who has been a wonderful
friend and steadfast support. Thank you for everything,
especially our two jewels, Madhuri and Namrata.

—Ram Mohan Menon

Contents

CONTENTS

Foreword

Sales and marketing are like the selection of the Indian cricket team. Everybody is an expert. Everybody has an opinion. And the official selectors are always blamed when the Boys in Blue don't do well. So, it's always nice when some genuine experts enlighten us on key aspects of sales management.

Roshan Joseph and Ram Menon are genuine experts. They have been there, done that and now are sharing their years of experience and success in the field.

Most Indian organizations are willing to invest a ton of resources and funds into R&D and manufacturing. And yet somehow, they do not invest enough thought into sales strategy and developing the function, although they often spend large sums of money in this area. Even when it comes to supply chain management, it's the backend supply chain that gets attention and focus. The supply chain management of the front end, that is, from factory to consumer gets short shrift.

In terms of sheer numbers, startup organizations are growing day by day (Angel tax issues notwithstanding). These startups are by people with varied backgrounds and skill sets. But all of them have one thing in common. They have a good idea. And this good idea is more often than not a good product or service. And all of them have read the adage of building a better mousetrap. The only problem is that no matter the quality of the mousetrap, consumers seldom beat a path to one's door. You have to reach the consumer.

In-between this nebulous consumer and the poor startup entrepreneur are layers of in-betweens and go-betweens, and filters and trade layers. Sometimes these layers are inhouse, and sometimes external. But they all have to be managed and handled. Be it trade channels, be it in house sales staff, be it e-commerce intermediaries or the franchised selling organizations, they all need to be managed.

The most difficult area in sales strategy and decision-making for a startup is not just what decisions to take among the various choices and options available. More important is what are the areas in which decisions need to be taken. Most startups have little idea on this area.

What this book does is lay it out for you. It tells you, above all else, what the questions are that need to be asked. And then goes on to suggest options and strategies depending upon each individual's own product peculiarities and criteria. To that end, this is an invaluable book for all startups.

In India, as in most of the world, operational sales management is not taught in most universities and business schools just like operational marketing management is not taught, but that's a different story. Consequently, most people in the industry, even those in sales-related areas, do not have the conceptual framework and sales management map to enable them to lower the learning curve. This book would be an invaluable primer for them. It won't help increase sales, but it will help them to ask the correct questions and seek the right answers. To that end, while this book is aimed at startups, its usefulness goes way beyond startups. This should become a useful learning tool for all sales managers and their business bosses.

Chief executives of existing organizations, who don't have a background in sales management, would find this book particularly useful as a checklist to ensure that they are asking the right questions and that their organizations are evaluating the correct matrices. It's surprising, the extent of silo-ization that actually exists. This book should help in breaking some of that.

What I liked about this book was also its ease of reading. Enough complexity to engage the specialist, and at the same time with an ease of reading to engage the non-sales background entrepreneur.

It explains concepts simply and gives options and suggestions in a way that does not talk down to the reader, but rather engages and challenges.

This is a book that is going to be read and discussed in fora well beyond the writer's target audiences.

I wish both Roshan and Ram all the very best in this endeavour. And I thank them for adding value to a very ignored area of management knowledge.

Kurush Grant

Preface

Nothing today is quite what it seems. With the tech tsunami at our doorstep, and with artificial intelligence matching human competence, there will be a new wave of startups that will rain down upon the market. In the last great dotcom bubble bust, thousands of hopeful startup entrepreneurs bit the dust. While some had technology limitations that drove them under, the majority of the companies were not able to handle the demand side of the equation.

Yes, it was the lack of an adequate sales and marketing competence that caused them to self-destruct.

The greatness of the USA economy is in the strength of small business enterprises. Data from 2016 shows that there were 5.6 million employer firms in the United States. Firms with less than 100 workers accounted for 98.2 per cent.

Interesting is to note the number of new enterprises that open each year. Approximately 627,000 firms open doors and probably occupy the premises vacated by the 595,000 that close down business each year. India is eyeing fast growth, and the move to incubate startup enterprises is a clear government policy. All efforts are underway to provide resources that will get such efforts on the road. Yet, little is offered as roadmap to commercial success.

The Startup's Guide to Sales has just one purpose. It is a step-by-step guide to build your own sales team. It stops avoidable mistakes and gives a clear path to successful selling.

The IITs and other institutes of excellence churn out thousands of wannabes who dream to be the next Gates or Jobs. Unfortunately, no one tells you how to sell the product you are so proud of. Reality sets in when a-begging one goes to the market. Sharks and vultures await the hapless hero.

Today with IT dominance, the face of modern retail has significantly transformed. E-commerce appears to be the only way forward. This would see many traditional trades disappear. New ones will appear.

The redoubtable 'mom and pop' were the ones that took the hit with the huge onset of supermarkets and hypermarkets. Interestingly enough, the nature of the store down the road has also changed. More of these little stores offer unique products or services that the megastores could not be bothered to stock. The joy of human interface is still an endearing quality that makes the shopping experience so personal.

There will always be a new idea. Enterprise is the lifeline of humankind, and there will be the need to sell your brilliant product in a new and special way. Sales teams, like the legendary mom and pop stores, will transform and return to serve the customer.

This is a simple book on how one goes about building a sales team from scratch.

This book answers all questions such as,

'Do I need a sales force and when do I not need it?'
'How do I hire a salesperson?'
'What should be the design of the sales channel?'
'Is training the sales team necessary, and what if they quit after training?'
'What is time and territory management?'
'What is an ideal cost to sales ratio?'

These and other such questions will be given straight answers, which will help guide decisions.

Over 43 brief chapters, sales wisdom of the ages has been laid out to ensure your effort is well directed and planned for success. It is written with simple instructions that, at times, are a simple checklist of the 'dos and don'ts'. Stick with the 'dos' and you will be fine. You will have the comfort that the new enterprise is confidently stepping out. To find a place under the market sun.

Section I

Do I Need a Sales Force?

Most of the time entrepreneurs are products or services focused and do not understand why the market will not welcome their new introduction. Is a sales force necessary for success? Yes and no. Can one do without it and yet meet the numbers? These are questions that each startup must answer.

1

What If I Sold on My Own?

How to allocate time for selling and utilize the core competency of entrepreneurs?

Congratulations! You have chosen the path of the startup entrepreneur. You must have had no choice. It is akin to falling in love. If it does happen, there is little room for any other option, despite all the sage warnings and well-meant cautions. The path of the self-made entrepreneur is long, arduous and demanding. Not for the faint-hearted.

The Entrepreneur

You have worked very hard to get your brilliant idea understood by your world and when the day finally came, there are still bugs to iron out. This moment is a monumental one: to see the prototype change into the real product. It truly is a 'proud parent' time.

You are technically sound and have worked out all the challenges of developing the product. You have nurtured your dream through every 'naysayer' and prophet of doom. Now is the moment of truth. Go to market. Easier said than done.

The Sales Challenge

This is the hardest part of the entrepreneur's experience. As much as you want to believe that your new product is the best thing that has happened to mankind since potato chips, the market may never see your product at all, unless you get the selling factor in place.

It gets even worse when there is no product in the market that is even close to yours. If your product is a Fast-Moving Consumer Goods (FMCG), it is easy to get people who will be able to move your invention to the final consumer. If it is unique, it gets harder to find a selling solution.

No One Understands Me

Worse, when it is your own sales team. Salespeople today are on a very sticky wicket. There is increasing fear that software and artificial intelligence will replace them. Few, if any, are willing to hazard their software dictated resume. A failed effort on a new and unknown product adds nothing to a fledgling resume.

Tara was an accomplished manager and her ascent to the top of the sales hierarchy was no surprise to those who watched her career. After years of selling branded products that were well accepted in the market, she was offered the chance to lead the sales effort in a startup company. It was a brand known internationally and had only launched in India a few years earlier. No one in India knew the brand. It was a totally unknown quantity.

The market reception was cold for an unknown brand. On her first day at work, she was told that more than half of all sales positions in the company were vacant as the attrition was high. Tara realized that the first action she had to take was to fill the empty slots. She contacted the HR who arranged for a slew of biodata and soon she was interviewing candidates to select. It took her about six weeks of earnest pursuit before she had all positions loaded.

Being a good sales leader, she ensured that a thorough induction was completed for all the recruits. Bright and early the following Monday, she released everyone into the market. Three of them did not return after the first experience of rejection they experienced. Tara was traumatized by this. Never had she experienced such a reaction. She realized that selling in a startup would be a different ball game altogether.

There is a happy ending to Tara's story. She did get on top of her game and soon there were many who wanted to join her sales team. When she finally moved on, every position in her team was loaded with sharp salespeople and the startup was a success.

Seeing your product being massacred in the marketplace increases the temptation to DIY (do-it-yourself). This is often not the solution when the entrepreneur is an intern in sales, or worse. Resource constraints often bring out the multitasker in you. However, there is logic in doing so if you are a master of the sales terrain. Or, it is a simple death sentence. All the years of harrowing product development come crashing down. To risk with inadequate resources in selling is not a prudent strategy.

David's Downer

Arrowhead EduTech was the passion, ever since David left engineering college. He dreamt that one day his skills in writing software would make him a household name in education technology. He wrote with great care an app that could be used by teachers all over the world to monitor the development of each student.

David worked day and night to iron out every glitch and bug that presented itself as the application was worked out. Coming from a long line of teachers, he demonstrated to all the revered aunts who were sceptical of these new-fangled efforts to change the tried and tested methods of teaching. However, when David showed them just how simple his app was to use, even they were impressed.

David was so sure of his product that he felt his personal effort was really needed to sell the app to schools. He also realized that no one salesperson would understand the technical aspects well enough to explain like he could. He decided to go at it on his own. He was sure that the orders would come rolling in.

It was when he hit the road that the problems started to mount. School authorities were difficult to contact and often it took him a whole day just to meet one school principal. He spent hours waiting for an interview. He also realized that decision-making was a slow process in the academia. He got a few orders. He found that working 24×7 was not enough. He soon had to be hospitalized after a breakdown. Arrowhead was never to be.

Challenge of the Bazaar

In all our years of consulting to entrepreneurs, young and old, we have never seen a project report of sales numbers being beaten in the field. Sure, project costs overflow budgets and quality parameters take time to be reached. In most cases, the production challenge is solved before the selling one is.

It is heartbreaking to see rows of beautiful products sitting patiently in depots, waiting for an order from the field. Immediately, all the spreadsheet numbers go out of sync. Unless the marketing challenge is overcome, the future is anything but rosy. Break-even keeps going farther away, a receding speck, in the uncertain horizon.

A client in agriculture nutrients, hastily put together a team of motley salespeople to push the new product to farmers. There was great push, strife and celebrations when, at year end, they had invoiced about ₹100 million of the fruit nutrients. By middle of the following year, the product returns started to happen. The shelf life was about eight months before it started to change into an opaque gel, unusable, even if the farmer was willing to use it. Chaos reigned when close to ₹60 million worth of products were returned from the market. They did not recover from this crippling blow.

Mastering Sales

As terrible as a sales disaster can be, there is no way to bypass sales. The only thing to do is to understand what it is all about. Something that this book will do, most efficiently. This book distils years of sales experience into simple easy steps. Read it with the knowledge that it will help you get your new startup on the road to success. Hold on to your seat.... We are ready to ride!

There is an old adage that says, 'What cannot be cured, must be endured'. Sales has to be endured. Doing it on your own is a passage to calamity, unless you have mastered the skills and have the experience. It is wiser to leave it to the experts and learn enough about sales to help you understand the challenges better. Even if you hire a super sales team, you need to know what they are doing and how to control strategy.

2

Why Not Use E-Commerce to Sell?

In this age of a billion-dollar sales through e-commerce, every startup would need to ask: Is selling online the right choice?

Given the options available today, there is always the temptation to plan on an online sales assault. The number of digital buyers worldwide is estimated to be around 1.92 billion in 2019. Every major retail giant is seeking a portion of the online pie. Walmart, the people who taught the world to retail efficiently, are also pushing their online platform. About 14 per cent of all US retail sales are digitally sourced.

It might appear as the most efficient solution. And it could well be. However, check if your product or service to be launched, is right for an online format.

How to Determine Fit?

A simple question to ask is does it need to be explained or is it a commonplace item. Most startup companies are innovative and hope to hit the market with something unique. If you have a hard time explaining what your product does for an average consumer, go easy on the online solution.

Online options are great if it is an everyday and common product. Also, if your products do not need to be touched, smelled or custom made. Many cosmetic brands have stayed away from online sales as they were considered only fit to be sold in the presence of a professional, who can advise on the correct way to sell. Bose, known for their fine sound systems, only lately have permitted online sales. It was felt necessary to be sold in conjunction with the delivery of customized advice.

Products that need to be explained, demonstrated and are dependent on a warm relationship between the customer and the salesperson are the best ones to stay away from online sales. It is a researched finding that as relationship grows, in a customer–salesperson association, sales too increase.

Benefits of Selling Online

There are definite advantages to be able to sell using some form of e-commerce.

1. There is a quick start. Once the basic platform is acquired, the shop is open 24×7×365 and business can get started. This takes much longer in the other system.
2. Low cost of operation is another attraction, given that this format works for you to meet targets.
3. Especially if you can piggyback some existing online system like Amazon, the increase in brand awareness will be working for you.
4. These mega platforms ensure footfalls which expand customer reach.
5. Product information can be well placed for the potent consumer.
6. Tracking your consumer is easy online and it helps to personalize the marketing effort.

There Are Pitfalls Too

Shipping costs can be underestimated, leading to upsets in the profit and loss account. Online sales require a 24×7×365 regime, and, if one does not respond quickly enough, the social media chatter could cripple an otherwise promising enterprise. Just because it is easy to sell anywhere online is no reason to do that. Start with a few products till the medium is mastered. Then go as you wish.

Products Most Likely to Succeed

Today all sorts of wonderful and weird products sell online. There are some guidelines to deciding which way to go.

The product must not be fragile. Typically, small packages get bumped and smashed in the process of shipping. Remember you are here to sell not to keep replacing damaged goods from irate consumers.

Software products are really made for this medium. It is possible to electronically ship software programmes and crash the transaction lead time.

Products that are perishable are not ideal for this medium. This can end up with messy inventory issues. Expired stocks are not fit even as manure.

Products that can be customized are a better fit, it also allows for better margins.

However, if your new startup has the uniqueness and ability to attract consumer interest, then you are well advised to go online. Remember that if there is any doubt about this, then choosing to go with a sales team is a safer option. This way of going to market is capable of making midway changes and avoid a do-or-die approach which online does practice.

The choice of setting up a sales team indicates a commitment to the long haul. It is so easy to make decisions for the current year. It gets increasingly harder, to look into the medium, and the long run. The results of developing a sales team are not immediately appreciated. Playing the finite game is sometimes headier and more exciting. Business is, however, an infinite race. Playing it well needs patience and commitment.

3

Can I Outsource Sales?

How important is it for a new product or service to have a captive sales force? There are strong arguments on both sides; however, it is again the nature of the product, available resource bandwidth and the commitment to a long-term solution that would determine the choice.

Many new companies, that enter the consumer goods category, piggyback on another sales network. There were such organizations many years ago, as setting up an independent organization was considered too expensive. There were distribution organizations such as G. K. Atherton and even Voltas that sold on behalf of their principals. Even today, in places such as Muscat in Oman, there are such 'distribution companies'.

The modern form of this is the Amazon and Flipkart versions that provide B2C facility to the struggling and successful startups. So, the question facing each startup is what should the model be.

Piggyback

When Amul first launched its milk products, the distribution was conducted through a 'selling agency'. Things went smooth initially. It later led to apprehension. This ended with a return to quarters for all players. In time, Amul found the critical mass and their legs, to plan distribution with the company's own sales team.

When Henkel was first launched in India, they sought distribution help from Eveready batteries that had a formidable distribution network. A number of brands of detergents were launched using the Eveready network. Finally, Henkel took over the distribution and continues to this day.

Owning a distribution network is a valuable asset. It comes with loads of issues that can sometimes be harrowing. This book tries to take the mystery out of the issue. Each chapter addresses some of the difficulties before the sales network gets ticking.

Products Define

For a startup, there is a need to carefully consider the amount of attention that the salesperson must give to get results. Products that are new demand more attention.

On the other hand, regular products without much technical details need much less support. Volume of goods sold and those that are gauged by revenue generated are not the best indicators of future potential.

Often the nature of the product requires detailed selling that incorporates technical features. Here too, the principle of sticking to the advantages that are most likely to ease the customer's pain will be the one to be chosen.

Stepchild Syndrome

The biggest danger in piggybacking is that new products with low revenue-earning capacity tend to be the neglected children. It is hard to get a salesperson excited about future potential when today looks so bleak.

This neglect is not useful for the startup.

While the cost of selling is an important criterion, it cannot be more important than effectiveness and performance. Especially, if the launch is a new concept, it is important to give the full support that only an exclusive sales team can give.

Frying Pan To...?

Omar was a bright young entrepreneur. He was an extraordinary student and had on two occasions won the science talent prize at high school. He was the first from his school to be selected to an IIT.

During the five years of rigour, Omar found time to innovate and, by his fourth year, had a working prototype of a solar torch. This lantern could solar charge the batteries with three hours of moderate sunlight so that it could work for 10 hours at a stretch. Omar understood how useful this could be for students studying into the night during power outages.

On graduation, he opted to skip placement and decided to cash in on his invention with a fellow IITian. Venture capitalists offered seed money, but they were uncertain about committing to a risk that they could not handle. They managed to produce limited quantities with hired facilities. They agreed that they would have to sell through a third-party sales team that was selling CFL bulbs.

Sales never took off. There was hardly any placement in stores. Outstanding payments grew. Quality complaints increased. Omar and partner declared bankruptcy and left for the USA for an MBA in Wharton.

If your own sales force is the way, then it is important to do it right. This guide will take you through all the steps to a successful startup. It is a fun ride. So, hold on.

4

Is Training an Essential Input for Sales?

Most startups do consider training. While this is a prerequisite, there is also a need for ensuring a uniform level of sales skills as most salespersons hired would be from a variety of industries and background.

So, you have decided to go with your own sales team. A good decision, until now. You have probably hired sales veterans and have naturally expected that all the team needs is a good short induction programme. Hand them brochures, price lists and samples and they could hit the road running. Nothing could be more wrong.

When a startup hires salespeople, it is more than likely that the team hired has never sold anything close to the product before. It is possible that they have visited the same customers, but not for the current product. Sales veterans you have hired could be from vastly differing companies and practice many ways to the market.

While hiring a veteran gives an added lift to your product, remember that the first gap to fill is the product knowledge. It does not help if the salesperson is iffy about the salient technical features.

Yogi Raj was an excellent salesperson working for Union Carbide. He was in the CPD(S) group that dealt with batteries and flashlights. At that time, the newly formed Agricultural Products Division (APD), making pesticides was having a tough time selling to the Indian farmers. Some bright spark in marketing felt there was potential to sell Sevin HP, a household pesticide, using the CPD network. Remember this was a sales team that never sold a pesticide.

It was not surprising that the launch was a flop. The product was effective against cockroaches. Late one afternoon, there was an enquiry from the Taj group of hotels for Sevin HP. The branch sales manager assigned Yogi to call on the Purchase Manager, Taj, Nikhil Swaminathan. Yogi was asked to identify the chemical composition of the Sevin HP. He stuttered, 'Sevin kills cockroaches'. It did not please Nikhil. He insisted on knowing the chemical composition.

A crestfallen Yogi went back to the sales branch and asked the branch sales manager the answer to Nikhil's question. The branch manager was no wiser. He said instead, 'Does he want to get rid of the cockroaches or fulfil his urge to be a quiz master?'

Making Things Clear

Just as important as it is to have full product knowledge before going to the customer, it is also important to make clear what is the official sales process to be followed by each sales team member. These guidelines have to be followed by all so that it becomes obvious to all customers that discipline is encouraged.

Equally important is to define the boundaries of what amounts to a healthy sale. Very often, in their urge to please, new recruits oversell, often making claims that are not true. This not only damages the product but also the equity of the company.

Define Action Steps

A common mistake made by those setting up a sales team for a startup is defining only the targets and not the strategy for meeting them. Without this, there can be orders but the launch process could be jeopardized. A signed order does not mean that the person buying it fully appreciates the limitations or even the scope of the features built in. Without this being clearly explained, there could be many avoidable disappointments.

Put Things Down on Paper

Veteran salespeople often prefer to keep things simple and store info in their heads. There is a need to write reports regularly. Attrition is increasing in all fields. It won't do any good to have your star salesperson walking away with all the confidential information tucked into the hat. It never does a harm to plan writing reports when the pressure eases up. It never does.

How Basic is Basic?

I am often asked this question: 'How basic should induction training go?'

The answer is simple: As basic as you can get. Do not presume that 'It is a well-known fact'. State and repeat so that there is no doubt remaining. Take nothing for granted. For instance, practice small things like the proper way to shake hands, handover visiting cards and even tell how to say goodbye.

Is There Something Called a Sales Process?

Each company must define the sales process and ensure that it is followed in every sales call. The sales process is a concise step-by-step guideline for how the salesperson must conduct the sales interaction. Starting from the first greeting, until the order is signed and payment made. Each industry can vary their sales process to suit the peculiar conditions. However, it is not useful to have a 'do whatever but get the order' policy to lead the sales team.

Startups must be extra careful as there may not be a standard sales process that might be right for the new launch. It helps to make a test market situation replicate the possible market conditions that might be faced. It is smart to get some advice in setting up an appropriate sales process.

Section II

Building an Effective Sales Force

Most startups would need an effective sales team to achieve their performance numbers. However, there are many decisions that may impact on how effective a sales force they will have. This is something that needs careful consideration.

5

Is Relevant Experience an Important Criterion for Selecting Sales Force?

Most startups are in a hurry to succeed in the market. While cutting down on incubation time is attractive, at times it can be counterproductive. To err and start again is both time consuming and expensive. Choosing well on this question makes all the difference in winning.

Is Relevant Experience an Important Criterion for Selecting a Sales Force?

There was a very experienced business manager called Avi, who had an impressive career working for a multinational company. After he retired, he caught the startup bug. He wanted an innings where he would be his own boss. He came up with an interesting product that would help people lose weight using Ayurveda potions.

It was tested and found to have no side effects. The treatment was for 3 months and thereafter, a yearly reinforcement. As there was no competitive product, it was hard to find salespeople from the industry. He had little capital and decided that he would take on salespeople with no experience. They are also cheaper to get.

His logic appeared sound. Being a first in the product market, he argued that even if he was to hire experienced salespeople, he still would have to teach them all aspects of the product. He felt the younger the salespeople were, the more they would be quick to move. Sadly, they were quick to move ... to other companies.

There is a thing to understand about young salespeople today. They are rarely engineered for disappointments and lack of success. A startup is often messy and there are frequent chances of greeting failure. There is a great concern today for employability. Gaps in one's biodata is what HR professional's lookout for. To explain a period of low success is a risk no one will take today. So they quit before they can fail.

Buy Experience

There is an old adage that works even today for startups. Get the team with a proven record. One that would withstand even a dip in the fortunes of the new business. Avi learned fast, he hired a number of experienced salespeople. It did cost him more. Yet, considering that the new team was able to make a huge success of his weight loss product, it really was the wise decision.

This applies to not only sales, but every new project. The mental makeup needed for a startup is quite different from the one, in a running safe business. This is why the star salesperson from a stable and leading diesel generator company was a misfit when it came to dealing with a product that was low in brand equity. The company he had joined was no. 3 among the major DG set brands.

It got so bad that he had to face the humiliation of not having cracked a sale in over 4 months of his joining. The easier decision was to quit before being asked to do so.

When a new company starts to lose its sales team, it reflects poorly on the brand and on those who deal with it. The product being new is an obstacle that every salesperson must surmount. Add to this, the sight of sales team members running away from their assignments. That can be disconcerting, to say the least.

Hiring the right personnel for your sales team could make all the difference, between success and bombing in the market.

6

What Are the Skills and Competencies Desired in a Salesperson?

While gentle prodding is always useful, self-starters are good for startups. How does one gauge attitude while selecting a salesperson? Sales mavericks can sometimes do severe damage. A fine balance is highly desired.

The interview to hire a salesperson is never satisfying. Today there are websites whose purpose is to help the candidate put on 'the best face'. This makes it harder to separate the wheat from the chaff.

How Does Wheat Look?

A salesperson has to be an optimist. So how does an optimist look? There are no reliable ways to spot an optimist. It is believed that the first salesperson was hired the day a consumer said 'no'. Traditionally, there had always been shortages and it was the supplier who used the word 'no'. With the rapid ease of manufacturing, it soon became the turn of the consumer to say the depressing words 'no, I don't want it'.

Dr No, I Presume?

Essentially, the major task of any salesperson is to get the consumer to review the 'no' and turn it to a 'yes'. Just as people who are unwell visit a doctor and come away with potions that make them well; similarly, the salesperson is a doctor adept in changing a negative into a positive. A real Dr No.

Gloom or Doom?

When the salesperson enters the room, how does he make you feel? That is important. A salesperson who can walk in and make the customer feel good about the morning is something to look out for.

Don't just focus on the glib answers given but also on the speech and if that improves the atmosphere in the room? An adept salesperson will weave the topics to answer all the difficult questions you have lined up, however, there would be much illumination at the end of the tunnel.

Not Just What, But How

So, in a sense, 'what is said' has precedence over 'how was it said'. We cannot ignore if what was said was said with some effect or impact. That is what a salesperson needs to do: Say things that will have an impact on the consumer's buying decision.

However, there is more to a salesperson than mere learning to speak well.

Is There a Plan?

Speaking, even gibberish, with a plan, can make a lot of sense. The professional salesperson will have a plan to get you to say 'yes'. Otherwise, a belief in good luck would hardly do, as a plan. Prayer, it is reported, has had greater benefit among those salespeople inclined to be pious.

The plan is yet another way to say if there is any strategy.

Any Plan 'B'?

Most salespeople face unforeseen difficulties in their quest for the sales order. When things don't go right, what is the way out? How does the salesperson think when on a hotspot? This can be checked by simply changing the interview to a session when ambiguity is introduced. Ask a question like: 'Your flight is 2 hours late and there is no charge in your cell phone, no bookstore open and all the food outlets are closed for a labour general strike. What would you do?

Here is when Plan B applies.

Seek Stamina

There has to be proof of being able to take physical hardship. The salesperson who wilts is the one who will have a hundred reasons for not achieving the target. Recall the salesperson calling in the office to tell the boss, it's raining too heavy to be out selling. The sales manager responds, 'Buy an umbrella, and continue selling'.

Beyond the JD

One important criterion for choosing the right salesperson is the willingness to go beyond the job description and be willing to support the team. If you expect to form a team of loners who seek only their goals, it will be a sad sales team. And poor results.

7

What Should Be the Size of My Sales Team?

VS.

Lean is the best. But it is always advisable to start with what you can handle and grow with the market.

The cost of setting up a sales team is not anymore a trifle. Care must be taken that, at all times, the control on the team's working is tight.

Cutting Your Coat

For a startup, it is important that one realizes that all the fish in the sea are not your customers, yet. There are tried and tested methods of using the reliable Pareto principle to define the most important of your prospects first.

While there are pressures to hit the market running, speed is not the priority but doing it right the first time. We recommend hiring just 1–2 salespersons initially to test the waters. It is imperative that the owner(s) of the startup accompany the salesperson on the initial days when customers are to be visited. Delegating this to anyone else is hazardous. Remember, no one knows your product better than you do. It is important to observe the response of customers to the first revelation of the new product or service being provided.

The All-Season Salesperson

There is no such salesperson available in the market. Ignore those who promise you an off the shelf, ready to sell salesperson. If your product is not a common FMCG one such as soap or toothpaste, you need to invest in creating your specific hit team. The time spent sharpening your sales harpoon will be richly rewarded in performance.

In the following chapters, we will elaborate the critical information needed to net the customer in. This needs your involvement at the early stages of the sales process.

Time and Territory

The size of a sales team is dependent on the workload of each salesperson. The mistake often made is not to consider that there are about 26 days of market work each month. There must be defined work for each of the days or one can end up hiring salespeople who moonlight.

There was this importer of high-end electrical goods and he hired salespeople to go about selling the products into a metropolitan city. Being high-end and newer technology, there were not more than a handful of interested dealers. How often does one visit six dealers in a month? Understanding that their visits were not welcomed, in such frequency, each of the salespersons either stayed home or picked up alternate work that could occupy them for the balance period of time. In such cases, even one salesperson can be too large a sales force.

Peripherals of a Sales Team

Today, merely booting up a sales team has a number of concerns. There is a need to fit them with laptops, demo kits, catalogues, cell phones and possibly a company uniform. Each salesperson does have a cost such as salary, incentive and others; there is also a monthly expense of the touring salesperson: intercity and intracity travel, hotel accommodation and food. It is also prudent to cover them with medical and accident insurance.

After incurring all the overhead of a sales team, it is necessary that they are fully skilled to enter the market and be the catalyst to the customer buying in to the concept.

8

How to Conduct the Recruiting Process for Hiring a Salesperson?

Hire a person on the basis of both eligibility and suitability. For eligibility, one could look at qualification and experience. For suitability, one needs to consider issues such as how will this guy fit in this company, what is his overall attitude in the market. Based on these two aspects, the hiring process should be defined.

The best referrals come from word of mouth. However, the scale of your startup could require more than what word-of-mouth can supply. At times like these, it is wiser to go for a competent manpower placement agency. Most of them charge anything above 8.33 per cent of the annual CTC. It is worth it, if they can give superior manpower.

Hiring Process

The agency will shortlist the most potential candidates and do all the work to ensure they are on time for the interview. Interviewers at times are as nervous as the candidate. We need to lay a few ground rules.

Are we here to select or to eliminate? Interviewers sometimes feel that rejecting a candidate is a sure way of getting the best of the pick. The quest is to find those most apt to work as a team and bring in sales results.

Eligible and Suitable

These terms are well worth remembering. They are simple to recall and work well when considering anyone for a position.

There are two aspects of a person that make for a correct placement. This has been one of the guiding principles at Cadbury UK. Use the eligibility criterion to eliminate and the suitability one for selection.

Eligibility

Eligibility simply means a certain standard of education or experience that is necessary to comprehensively do a job. For instance, certain jobs require a level of technical education, be it a degree in mechanical or computer engineering.

Or a simple experience eligibility such as, must have done farming. Those who don't have the terms of eligibility don't make the interview. The manpower agency would have taken care of this. So, the purpose of the interview is essentially to check the suitability of the person for the assignment.

Suitability

The criteria for this is not clear. If the position is a leadership one, does the candidate have a pleasing personality? More than that, is the candidate someone who could be comfortable to deal with on a day-to-day, year-to-year basis? Likeability is not to be downplayed. So many employees get sacked finally not because they are not performing but because they are just a pain to work with.

Who's Suitable?

How does one find who's suitable? Hiring is not the same as courtship, when the subtle art of dating indicates who is and is not suitable. This is a hard one. Yet not so difficult if one relaxes the format of the interview and merely chat with each other, touching on topics dear to the candidate. As the atmosphere loosens up, defences are down and there is possibility to get to understand the candidate from a likeability factor. Certain companies shortlist and invite the select candidates to a leisurely meal. In a different format, they can assess if the persons selected are team players and exhibit any signs of selflessness. This is a good ingredient for team-building.

The Probation

The real proof of the pudding comes in the field. Veteran salespeople speak of how a day in the market is enough to assess what makes a salesperson tick. Do not just spend a morning in the market with the new recruit. Take the effort to work the full day.

Observe especially the energy levels at the end of the working day and the ability to display patience. Remember that extending probation is a sign of poor sales leadership of the boss not the person being appraised. If one is not able to figure out if a person is suitable at the end of the probation, ask the salesperson to go and leave the organization in no doubt.

Yes, it is tough to get good salespeople. Compromising helps no one.

Section III

Is Training of Sales Team Necessary?

Most startups choose a sales team with relevant experience. This requires a serious application of training to ensure all members of the sales team communicate a similar message. Induction and sales training are essential.

9

What Are the Skills to Be Imparted?

There are two separate areas of training: the first being technical which is to know your product and the second is the skill of selling which is how to understand your customer needs. Most startups believe technical training is enough, but the reality is that good selling skills make it easier.

Most salespeople have never had sales training. Teaching your new recruit about your product, pricing and promotion is often mistaken for sales training. Let's get this straight. Being master of your product is essential. However, learning how to sell is quite a different arena of training.

Technical Training

However simple or intricate a product is, it is always the hero. Knowing the product with all its myriad ramifications is always a challenge. The salesperson has no authority to step into the market without mastering the features, advantages and benefits of the product and how it matches competition.

Product pricing, dealer margins and all commercials important to the customer buying the product are all essential. Application of the product and every caution in use has to be a knowledge vital to the working of the product. Certain salespeople substitute as service engineers, so well do they know their product. This still does not ensure that a sale can be made.

Sales Training

Even if you hired a senior salesperson from the industry, it is quite likely that the person would be deficient in the process of selling. This separates the professionals from the amateurs. Amateurs too can get orders. It has to be on their lucky day. A well-trained salesperson seeks to close sales by using a proven sales process. It is rare that he will miss a sale. Even on unlucky days.

Understanding Needs

The professional salesperson is skilled in the system of making a sale. Exploring and identifying needs is a major difference between the trained and unsullied. Often there is no definite identification of the customer's needs. In such an event, there will be a hit and miss chance of getting the sale.

Principled Selling

Every professional selling system must perchance be well rooted in principles from which the sales process draws strength.

While there is no letting go on the drive to sell more, it is necessary to define what poor selling is; this should be put in a clear statement. Selling beyond the assessed needs of the customer is tantamount to sales malpractice. To be shunned at all costs.

A worthy sales leader understands what it means to push for sales and when to hold back. Often the sales pressure is so formidable that it takes a Herculean effort to hold back on sales.

John Chiu is an ex-pat sales head of one of the large banks of Oman. Despite his lack of experience in the Middle East, he quickly laid out the plans for growth and the limiting guidelines for when to stop. His team sold loans to high worth individuals. Yet, his instructions were unambiguous. Do not sell 'one rial' more than the assessed need of the customer. John set amazing records for loans given. All because he set clear guidelines and was unwavering.

Need for System

A well-developed sales process training takes care of all aspects of serving the customer. There are different types of customers all requiring attention for various needs. Salespeople who are better tuned to their customers' needs rarely miss much. Once every one in the sales team uses the same sales process, there is a definite sense of working together.

Sales training helps everyone sell more, even the superstars. However, putting in place a robust sales system ensures that new superstars emerge. Even the laggard in a sales team, if practicing the sales process, will produce results that will be sufficient to meet set targets. This is the biggest help an organization gets when the average productivity goes up, not just the sales of the top players.

10

What Are the Basic Selling Skills?

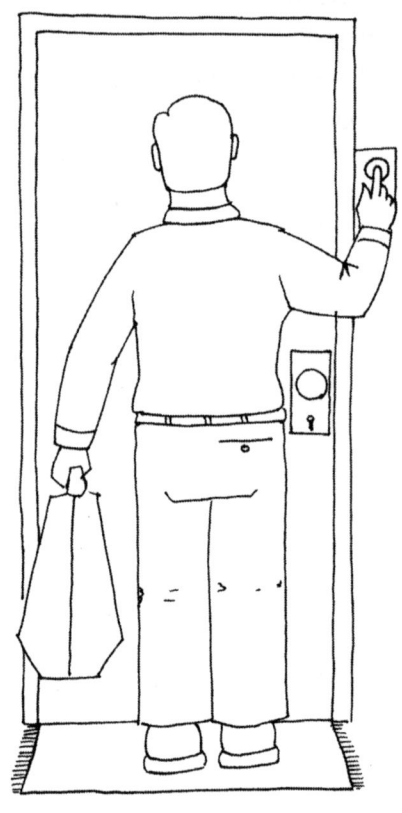

The first and most important skill is to care for your customer. Care enough to identify the real needs and be certain not to oversell. It is essential to know how to deal with objections, handle irate customers and learn how to pitch for results.

The Basic Selling Skills

A new sales recruit into the world of sales is often given a detailed induction to the company and its products. The sales training part is left to an on-the-job training (OJT), mainly by observation, of one of the senior salespersons who is supposed to mentor.

Incidentally, the senior salesperson too never had any formal sales training and has learned by observation. This tradition of handing down knowledge and skills from one generation to another is a common sales training convention.

Except, no one has had any framework of what a selling process is all about.

Skills of Selling: Relationship Building

Basic to any understanding of sales is a simple concept: If there is a sales force, there will be relationships that make or mar the sales transaction. The overwhelming logic is that 'better the sales relationship, better the sale'. This is a way of saying, the salesperson who has a strong relationship with the customer eventually has a better understanding of the operating reality of the customer's situation and will be better able to zero in on what will make the customer say 'yes' to a sale.

Skills of Selling: Customer Success

One of the widely used terms in management is to seek 'customer satisfaction'. This is no doubt a valid objective. In sales, the truly successful salesperson seeks to ensure the customer's success which will happen as a result of the purchase being made. It is known that a majority of the salespeople are only concerned about bringing home the sales order, often with no thought for the hapless customer.

Skills of Selling: Identifying the Gap

Crucial to professional selling is the skill of using exploratory skills to assess why the customer will need to buy the new product. Especially in the case of the startup, there is a good chance the product and its benefits are unknown to the customer. Here, the role of the salesperson is vital. The salesperson has to understand the operating reality of the customer and then figure out if there is a possible need for the product.

Having done that, the next part of the responsibility is to get the customer to realize their need. Unless this is accomplished, there will be little chance of a sale.

Skills of Selling: Making the Pitch

Having successfully identified the customer need, the next skill is the ability to present to the customer a coherent presentation that outlines the need, as realized by the customer, and how the new product provides a unique solution to the problem faced. If this is done effectively, and any objections raised, handled, then the sales order is a happy consequence. Both for the buyer and the seller.

Skills of Selling: Sell As Much As the Need

Sales is an infinite process, although each month end marks a painful finite closing. Yet the firm is not just for the month. As each month pulls along, the memory of the previous month's achievements become a bit vague. The customer is the final judge of the effective skills possessed by the salesperson. Selling in excess of the customer's need is clearly wrong, and doing it relentlessly is a case of sales malpractice.

Companies across the world have identified rogue selling as a serious damage to not only their sales but also to the brand equity. Many companies are proceeding legally to punish such salespeople. No one is helped when such irresponsible sales are conducted.

11

How to Make a Presentation?

This chapter emphasizes that the best of a pitch to a customer happens when there is clarity about customer needs that are both functional and personal. Without this, no pitch can be effective.

Little Ramesh was the favourite of the family and his baby talk made everyone wonder how he developed his vocabulary. He tended to talk endlessly. His father's brother, Uncle Ajoy, predicted that Ramesh would make a great salesman. This intrigued Anousha, his older sister; she quizzed Uncle Ajoy as to what made him say such a thing. 'He has the gift of the gab', said the proud uncle.

The Pitch

'The gift of the gab' seems to be the universal way to define the trait of a successful salesperson. It is unfortunately not the requirement of a professionally qualified salesperson. There is no doubt that there are many an order lost because the 'pitch' made just did not hit the mark.

There is a definite logic in ensuring that the pitch is correctly planned and delivered. There is more power in the logic of the presentation rather than just the manner of how the pitch was made. Just mouthing off a string of advantages does not really mean anyone has been convinced.

Is it then more important to get our pitch right than be concerned about the various aspects of effective communication? People train themselves to speak with appropriate voice modulation, accent and use of appropriate language. Perhaps if a little more emphasis was placed on working out the pitch strategy, there would be a better closing ratio.

Needs, Needs and Needs

Sometimes a good pitch starts very early in the sales process, not just at the time of asking for the order. The role of the salesperson is to meet the customer and ask questions that will reveal the operating reality of the customer. There is a need to answer the question: What is the overwhelming reason for a consumer to consider buying our product?

The Bullseye

The way to a pitch, which will have the requisite punch, is in the core of the presentation. Has the need relevant to the customer been identified? Does the solution designed by the company really fit the needs identified? If it does not fully fit, there will be some hesitation about placing the order. Or even a refusal to go with the order.

The Pitch Logic

A long-standing thumb rule which professionals adhere to is the 'rule of three'. This is an understanding of effective communication. The learning goes like this: For a message to be absorbed, there is a need to repeat it at least thrice. Any less, and there is a danger that the message could get missed or misunderstood.

The Rule of Three

Once the customer realizes his needs, there is a willingness to fill the gap by the customer. To pitch effectively, the salesperson must first restate the needs identified earlier on and proceed to give the solution. This is the best technique of pitching.

If the work of identifying needs is correctly done, there should be no reason for missing the order. Remember, the role of a great salesman is to help the customer make the correct buying decision. That decision has to give him profit. He must feel that the help of the salesman was crucial to his deciding well.

12

How to Ensure On-the-Job Training?

Every salesperson in a new job has a learning curve before he is ready to be left to work independently. His progression must be mapped and supported.

As important as classroom training is to the complete orientation given to the new salesperson, the work done on the job is what fortifies the learning. This is really important. It can make all the difference to the results in the market.

OJT: How to Do It

Most companies send the recruit out into the field along with the senior salesperson. Normally, this senior person has a sound and solid reputation for integrity. For a startup, there is no senior salesperson. It is advisable that the promoters themselves go the market to ensure no slip between 'the cup and the lip'. It is no use moaning about how the salesperson damaged the sales by doing wrong or poor sales.

Create Formats

While many things can be kept informal, OJT must be worked with recording all the observations made as the salesperson. Formats are called for.

Every visit made to a customer, the parameters on which the observer will note the performance of the salesperson is defined and informed before the visit. Care must be taken to allow the new salesperson to take the role of piloting the call. The observer would, if possible, make notations on the format sheet. It helps to take the permission of the customer before doing this.

Kerbside Counsel

On completion of the call, the observer should sit down with the salesperson and review all that was done well and also note down anything that was not up to the mark and had to be corrected.

I Like, I Wish

In doing the kerbside review, be sure to use the tried and tested method called 'itemized response'. By using this method, there is every possibility of facing a balanced response. This proven technique is effective even at home, dealing with parents, young children and other challenges.

This people skill creates a sound basis for negotiation and setting up a basis for understanding. This skill allows for acknowledgement of the good work done before one looks at areas of improvement.

Ken Blanchard, the famous management guru, had this to say, 'We managers have trained ourselves to catch people doing anything wrong.' He says, 'We now need to train managers to catch people doing things right.' Acknowledging what has been done well is as important to note as the errors made while doing a job.

A number of corporates have tried this itemized response skill of dealing with team members, and there has been an excellent response and a noticeable improvement in civility.

Once there has been a strong input of OJT, the sales team will be ready for the market.

Section IV

How Good Do You Want to Look?

A salesperson is the first impression that your customer gets of the company. How good do you want to look at this very critical moment. You don't get a second chance to make a first impression.

13

How to Present Oneself in the Market?

The appearance and energy with which your startup is presented in the market is a vital factor, especially since there is no branding support. Grooming of your sales personnel is an important addition to the first impact that is made.

Amrish was a charming personality and well liked by his team. In his role, he was often visited by the sales development teams from many vendors. There was an open secret that if the vendor consisted of good-looking ladies, Amrish would personally deal with them.

However, the team joked that if the vendor sent male salespeople, Amrish's assistant, Raju, would be asked to handle them. It created some curiosity when Amrish asked Raju to meet a particularly fetching young lady, who was to visit the office later that morning. Word went around in the department that this was a first: Amrish refusing to meet a good-looking business development manager.

Raju could not contain his amazement and blurted out: 'Boss, are you feeling okay today? How come you are allowing me to meet her?'

Amrish's response was short and cryptic, 'She has body odour.'

These situations do happen. How sensitive are salespeople to such obstacles that block us in the market?

Appearance

Being face to face with the customer requires special preparation. Consider the way airline stewardesses take great effort to be presentable. There was a time when the airlines was defined by the presentability of the cabin crew. The 'Singapore Girl' is another way of saying Singapore Airlines.

The hospitality industry understands this caution well. Sometimes, sales teams in other industries are too busy selling to worry about such little details. This could cost them in sales loss and they may not even be aware of that. Every human interaction has an appearance factor. Professional salespeople understand this and work it to their advantage.

There are simple tools of the appearance trade: a comb, which is readily available; a hanky or face tissues kept within reach; a small bottle of deodorant and a mouthwash can also be part of the sales kit. Customers today are more conscious of such issues, especially hygiene.

Energy

People like to do business with those whom they like. The likeability factor unfortunately cannot be induced in the timeframe that is available to the startup. This is a factor that must be ensured at the time of selection. Better to hire a pleasant personality rather than try to develop it in a naturally moody person.

Energy is at times simplified to mean hiring young sales team members. This is not necessarily true. As a startup, it is advisable not to recruit freshers. However, if hiring veterans is the plan, do select those who exude energy and a positive outlook.

Attitude

This is a vital part of likeability. Here too, it is not possible for a startup to mould a negative attitude in to a positive one. It might be possible to address this when the organization is well established. The process of changing a negative to a positive is time-consuming and fraught with complex issues.

There is also a possibility of the leader of the startup injecting a positive atmosphere by the sheer dint of entrepreneurial skill. At times, the inspiration of a committed leader gets transferred to the team, and lambs turn to tigers. This helps create a positive contact with the customers.

14

How to Make a Positive Contact at Every Interaction with the Customer?

The need to have a customer in the right frame of mind to listen to a salesperson forms an important part of how your message is received. There are techniques to help get the customer into the right mood.

The first time you see the customer's face, there is every possibility that he does not like what he sees. This is why a lot of work has gone in to ensure there is no apparent reason for a shallow rejection: the salesperson is well dressed, preferably in uniform. The hair is well combed and there are no offensive odours either.

The Greeting

The first task of the salesperson is to ensure that the customer is in a mood to listen to him.

There is a good amount of sales literature, which suggests that the greeting must be precise, happy and engaging. Even a 'good morning' can be said with feeling. The salutation has to be followed by a short capability statement. This effort to let the customer know which company is being represented and what is the business they are in can go something like this:

Good morning!
I am Ajoy, from B-More Consulting.
We are in the business of developing sales performance, installing effective sales teams and sales systems.

Then What?

What do you say after 'Hello'?

Here is the tricky part. This is where the salesperson has to take charge. Sales experts recommend that the initial conversation should be 'off syllabus'. In other words, don't get right into business. Start a conversation that would be in the interest of the customer. This could be about sports, world news or anything of general interest. You would avoid refocusing the customer's mind to what is of interest to you.

The topics must be of some interest to the customer. If you know he is a Chelsea fan, you might want to ask his views on how Chelsea was doing that football season. That would set him off talking. When he's finished, the time is right to get down to the work at hand.

Before stepping into the customer's office, plan your approach. Think of topics that you could take up. Look around and see if there is anything that could start a conversation. Go over the purpose of your visit. Keep a Plan A and a Plan B, in case there is something unpredictable that may happen.

Positive Contact, Each and Every Time

A question often put is that while positive contact is necessary, is it required to keep using the positive contact, each time that the customer is being contacted. There should be no difference between the first-time call and the regular call. In fact, the more grave danger is when one imagines there is no need to be so 'formal' and things, get lost all of a sudden.

It is vital that every customer call starts with the effort to put the customer in the right mood to discuss the business for which he is being visited.

What If He Has a Headache?

Despite all your best efforts at creating a positive mood, the customer appears sullen, pre-occupied, addressing phone calls and even goes out to confer with colleagues. It surely does not seem like a good day to make the call. What is the best course of action?

To carry on regardless is merely completing the action for statutory purposes. Perhaps, seeking another date might be a better strategy. Another time, another day will only improve the chances of cracking the order. When the customer is not in the mood, don't push it.

15

How Does One Start a Meeting and Follow a Template for Success?

VICE PRESIDENT

A professional meeting with the customer needs to follow a basic plan of how the salesperson will identify the customers' needs and how a solution can be offered.

A sales call has to be always planned in detail, if we hope to make it a productive call.

The Objective

If one is serious about selling professionally, the call objective must be written down clearly. This may appear as unnecessary, but, if one is a beginner in a sales territory, one cannot be taking anything for granted.

To achieve this goal, it is important that a sound strategy be outlined. The real outcome will be reflected in the strategy. Detailed action steps must be listed to ensure that the goal is met.

Sales Strategic Plan

If one is visiting the customer for the first time or the hundredth, there is only one immediate objective, as far as the salesperson is concerned: To dig deep and identify the needs of the customer.

Needs (Again)

Often, it is the salesperson who is expert enough to locate a customer's needs. The task is a little more difficult when the customer is yet to realize the needs applicable. It is the responsibility of the salesperson to explain to the customer how his satisfaction would be at the maximum and his profitability highest by deciding on the solution being offered. There is only one way to do 'need' mining: Ask the right questions.

Questions, Questions and Questions

The template to follow when a customer call is about to start: As always, it should be with a positive mood-lifting contact, followed by a series of questions that help in capturing the needs. There are five types of questions that help, and these should be sequentially followed.

General Information Question

This is the first of the series that should be asked in the first visit. Here the customer is encouraged to explain the nature of the business and the goals. Customers are more comfortable talking about their company and tend to relax. This is essential so that more specific information can be gathered from the client.

Drilling Down Question

Having gathered a general download on the nature of the business, it is time to turn to questions that are specific to the reason for the call. Here the customer is invited to share the experience with the current usage of the product. These questions will help to diagnose if there are any pain areas in the use of the competitor product.

The pain area is always a happy spot for the visiting salesperson. Excavating further, there is sure to be a latent need, if not an urgent one. Once the pain area is detected, there is need to dust around the object, like archaeologists do, to fully expose the need.

Valedictory Question

These are questions asked to test if the needs discovered are relevant to the customer. If the customer finds no depth in the findings, the process has to be redone so that the needs are confirmed.

Once both the customer and the salesperson have agreed on a set of needs, then the journey to a sales order is much easier.

Steve Jobs Question

In startup products, this type of question will become necessary. The products of startups are rarely 'me too' ones. Just as Steve Jobs wowed his adulatory fans with his, 'And one more thing...' (Steve always kept his big surprises for after this opening line), so also the startup salesperson. 'What if I could offer you a solution that will take you to a new level of satisfaction?'

Once the needs have been established and the customer is willing to buy a solution, the sales order will be forthcoming.

16

What Business Etiquette Must Be Followed?

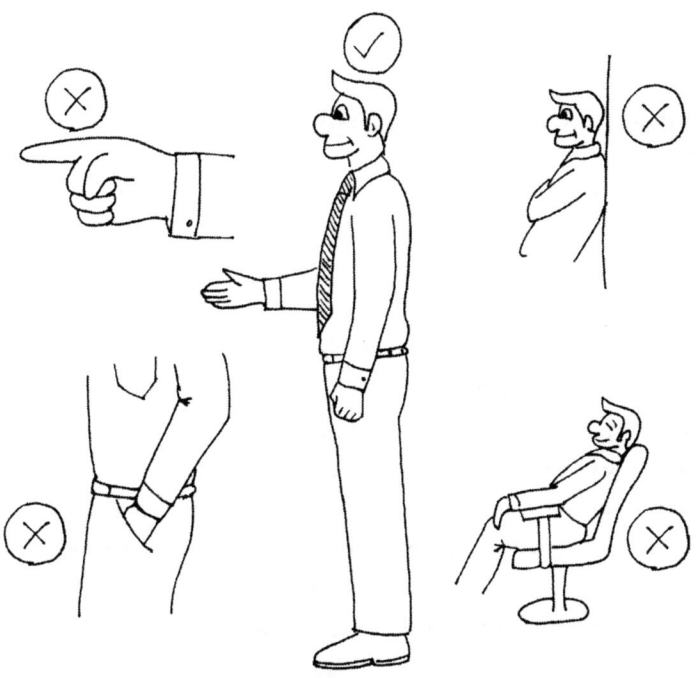

Today, there are global expectations of business etiquette regardless of where the customer is based. If the salesperson is unaware of the etiquette, a great deal of effort made to impress the customer would be wasted.

Business etiquette is always specific to a region. While there is worldwide acceptance of what is good business custom, many countries might find the traditions of other countries confusing, if not disturbing.

Greeting the Customer

To touch or not to touch is the question. Culturally, many parts of the world shrink from doing so. The Indian way is to greet from afar with a dainty 'Namaste'. Arabs rub noses, when not hugging each other with great warmth.

Within India too, there are levels of cultural fellowship. People of Tamil Nadu exhibit low tolerance of touching, hugging or even a lingering stare.

Contrast this with the people of North India. They are more effusive and have no hesitation in offering a burly hand in welcome. Dealing with women customers poses an even more tricky challenge.

In Muscat, it is not considered acceptable for strangers to shake hands with a woman. This might be a rule and women in banking and other sectors might be easy about mixing genders, yet one is never certain. To err on the side of caution is the safer option.

Shaking hands in greeting is a widely accepted mode. However, even in the shaking of hands, there are many unintended messages that might be communicated. If the handshake is not strong and vigorous, it might be construed as not welcoming enough. Sometimes a hand is proffered with no intention to squeeze. This is not received well. The hand should be firmly shaken not more than three times and then withdrawn.

Knock Three Times

Entering the customer's cabin has a courtesy. Knock three times firmly but not with impatience. Many stand at the doorway and ask, 'Can I come in?' This is not the correct way of asking. The appropriate question is 'May I come in?'

Do not presume to sit down in front of the customer, unless invited to do so. One could also seek permission to sit down with a 'May I sit on this chair?' Don't place anything on the customer's desk. It is not your space to occupy.

Most customers are hospitable and may offer you a cup of tea. Accept graciously, but remember to clear the used cups from the customer's desk. Don't imagine that there is a person to clear it. Leave the desk as clean as you first found it.

Taboo Topics

Never discuss politics, religion, family (unless you are well known to the customer) and any controversial topic.

Politics

Each person has the right to align with the party of his or her choice. Never try to convince the customer otherwise. It never works, and creates only fissures. Even if the customer has the same political preference as you, avoid any discussion, as you never know how things might go out of hand.

Religion

A person's beliefs are for the comfort of the individual and not for debate. A belief in a God, or in the absence of one, is every individual's choice. Nothing gives anyone a right to comment or criticize the belief of a person. This must be honoured at all times.

Family

A person's personal life is often separate from his business entity. Unless the customer speaks of his personal life, there must be no effort to probe there. Allow the customer to keep private whatever is considered personal.

17

How Important Is It to Be Punctual?

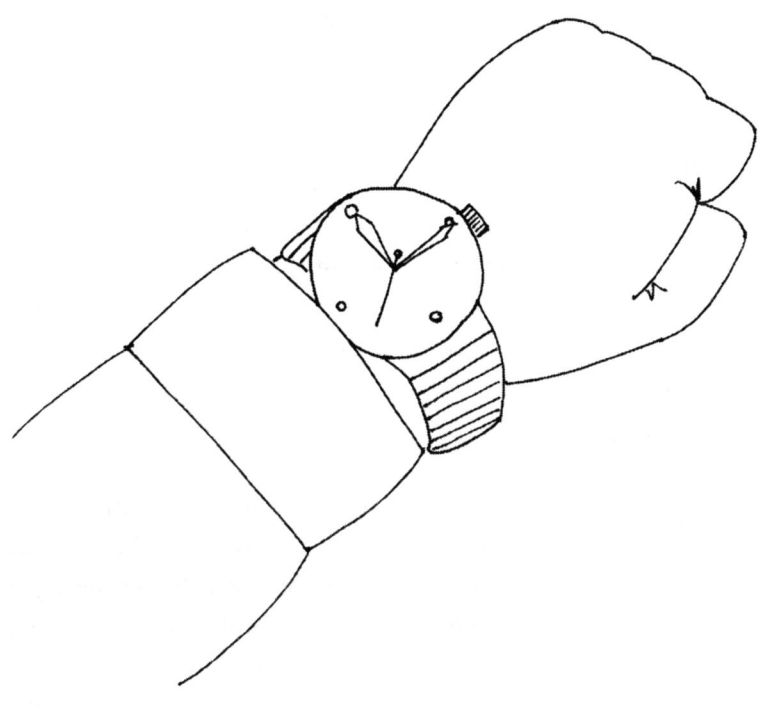

Being on time is only half the advantage. As your brand and company are unknown, it communicates quality and reliability that could be expected from you. How can one be on time, every time?

There are many reasons that will go to making your startup successful. Your product or service, pricing, promotion and the quality of your placement are among the many factors that contribute to this win. Your sales team, if they are professional in their work, adds greatly to the equity created.

Reliability

One of the most important aspects of servicing a customer is to project a value of reliability. Most businesses thrive when they are considered reliable. As the fortunes of the company sink, the major hit is on the reliability of the company.

Deadlines

Deadlines are the milestones of progress. As we pay attention to the deadlines, we get confident of progress. Meeting a deadline is what efficiency is all about. Being aware of the possibility of missing a deadline is as important as meeting one. The professional salesperson has the confidence to inform, sufficiently ahead of the expiry, that the deadline will be met late a few days. Naturally, this will evoke many an outburst. However, having been informed ahead of the schedule, those impacted can take evasive action.

Punctuality

Being on time has its own rewards. Sometimes there is an effort to justify being late. There are also attempts to make light of it and blame it on the DNA. The truth is it is a serious assault on a person's own brand equity. At times, this tendency of not being on time defines the worth of the person. The mark of a person.

Being late is, apart from the inconvenience, an insult to those who have been kept waiting. It shows a lack of character. It indicates that there is a strong streak of selfishness. And above all, it is a sign of not being reliable.

In this modern world, where trust is the basis of all commerce, this is the kiss of death for anyone seriously trying to build a place under the sun.

Punctual for life

In this world of doing more, there is always a good reason for missing a date. How does one still manage to keep being on time, all the time? It is useful to consider being on time as a process rather than an absolute. One can reset the appointment time, if running late, by calling up ahead of the meeting time. If this revised deadline can be met, you are still punctual.

Being ahead of schedule can improve effectiveness too. Reaching the meeting point, with time to spare, gives us the time to freshen up and review the notes one has for the discussions that will follow. The customer too would be impressed that you can be counted on.

It is hard to regulate life so finely that every step is bound by the time commitments we have made. Does a more easy focus on schedules help us lead a more relaxed life? Here's the secret. As long as the meeting timings are respected, there is enough time to let the hair down and enjoy taking it easy. Interestingly enough, keeping schedules is less stressful than suddenly having to drop everything to attend to the fire at hand.

Being on time creates more time for work or play.

Section V

What Should the Distribution Design Be? Is There a Method in the Madness?

The design of the distribution has a bearing on the number of salespeople that a startup must hire. There are many decisions that need to be taken so that the final consumer is satisfied with the product or service.

18

What Is the Difference between Distributor, Stockist and Wholesaler?

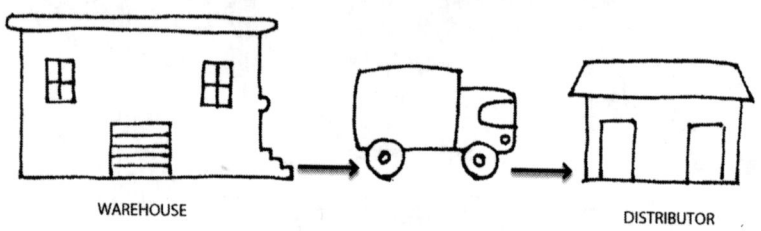

WAREHOUSE   DISTRIBUTOR

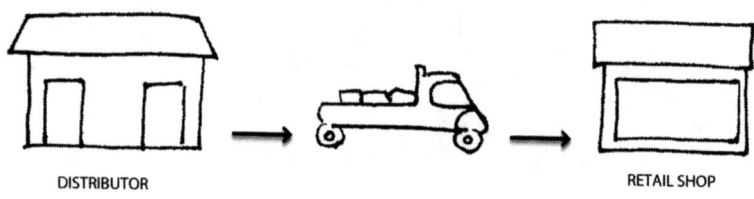

DISTRIBUTOR   RETAIL SHOP

It is important to understand the differences between various channel partners. Every tier of distribution created adds extra cost to the distribution model. When is it opportune to have a distributor, stockist and wholesaler?

The fundamental question that needs to be addressed by any business enterprise is how to reach the product to the end consumer. A few points that could aid in the process of deciding the distribution design are given below:

- Where do you expect the end user of your product to buy the product?
- How frequently do you expect the end user to buy your product?
- Where do customers of competitive products buy their goods from?
- How far is the source of supply of your product from the point at which the customer buys the product?
- What is the geographical area planned for the launch of the product in the short term and long term?
- Is the cost of transportation a significant factor in the final costing of the product and does it affect the decision on the distribution design?
- Is there a need for intermediate stock aggregation points such as warehouses to facilitate the movement of goods from supply point to final buying point?
- What is the frequency of refilling envisaged at these stock aggregation points?
- Does the product have a limited shelf life that requires to be considered while deciding on the distribution design?

The above are a few of the typical questions about the nature of your product, the location of sourcing point and where the product is to be sold. Apart from this, cost factors would have to be considered to make a well-informed decision. All these factors would be required to arrive at the ideal distribution design.

The next step would be to get an overview of the options available in the system to enable selling your product in the most efficient manner. Broadly, there are two options of selling: direct selling and indirect selling.

Direct Selling

- Online sales platforms, such as Amazon, where the supplier sells products with minimal intermediaries
- Exclusive brand outlets where the supplier sells products through company-owned or franchise outlets across target markets
- Single-level marketing like Eureka Forbes or multilevel marketing like Amway are examples of distribution channels that reaches products directly to the home of the end user
- All the above options could have stock aggregation points to facilitate faster deliveries

Indirect Selling

- Involves the use of intermediaries who buy and sell your products at a desired profit margin (PM)
- Intermediaries operate under various names—distributor, stockist, wholesaler, retailer (These are discussed in brief in the chapter.)
- Intermediaries could operate at one level or at multi levels depending on the needs of the product and the customer

Distributor

This intermediary's primary role is to widely distribute the company's products in the area(s) assigned to them. The distributor earns an agreed-upon margin on the sales of the products. So the selling price of the distributor is as per company recommended prices. Guidelines for operating as a distributor:

- Be the authorized representative of the company in the area assigned for all the products of the company
- Maintain the agreed-upon inventory level for each category of product
- Facilitate the implementation of market promotion campaigns as required by the company
- Refrain from being the distributor of competing products
- Sell products at the agreed-upon price to as many points as possible in the area specified by the company
- Products could be sold to next level of intermediaries such as to wholesalers and/or retailers
- Invest in selling supports such as vans, motorcycles that aid in distribution of products
- Hire salespeople to sell company's products in the area assigned
- Ensure that agreed-upon payment terms are adhered to
- Ensure that agreed-upon credit terms are offered in the market

The company in turn needs to ensure that the distributor earns the expected return on his investments. This could be achieved through offering the desired margin on sales, reimbursing distributor expenses towards sales team, van operations and ensuring that inventory levels do not exceed the expected norms.

Stockist

The primary role of this intermediary is to stock and sell company products that are required by retailers located in the local markets. The orders booked by salespersons visiting retailers of a given market are supplied by the local stockist. They are rarely expected to sell in markets beyond their own local market and hence are not expected to make additional investments for distribution of products. The stockist earns an agreed-upon margin on the sale of the products. So the selling price of the stockist is as per company recommended prices.

Guidelines for operating as a stockist:

- Be the authorized representative of the company in the area assigned for all products of the company
- Maintain the agreed-upon inventory level for each category of product
- Supply the orders booked by salespersons visiting the retailers of the market
- Supply the orders raised by retailers of the market from time to time
- Sell products to retailers of the market at the agreed-upon price
- Products could be sold to the next level of intermediaries such as wholesaler and/or retailer
- Ensure that agreed-upon payment terms are adhered
- Ensure that agreed-upon credit terms are offered in the market

Wholesaler

This intermediary is very different, as they are not appointed by the company unlike the distributor or stockists who are appointed by the company. This difference determines their guidelines of operation of their business. Wholesalers are independent traders buying, stocking and selling a range of goods as per their assessment of the market demand for the products.

Guidelines for operating as a wholesaler:

- Buy, stock and sell products in demand from retailers who visit their shop

- Aim to achieve high volumes in business by operating on minimal margin
- Their business model is based on the principle you buy at lowest price and sell at lowest price
- Aim to be the lowest cost source of supplies for all retailers visiting their shop

Retailer

This is the final intermediary—a point from which the end user buys the product. Retailers are independent traders and are not appointed by the company. The primary role of a retailer is to stock and sell a wide range of products of various companies as per expected demand from end users located in the markets. They serve the demands of customers who visit their retail outlet.

In certain industries, the company sells directly to such points that sell to end users. In such a case, the points that sell directly to end user are also known as dealers.

Guidelines for operating as a retailer:

- Buy, stock and sell products as per demand of buyers who visit their retail outlets.
- Display products in retail outlets to enhance sale of products stocked.
- Participate in market promotion campaigns introduced by the company.
- Margins earned by retailer are far higher than that of distributors, stockists or wholesalers to compensate for their investment in high-cost location of their outlets and stocking of inventory for long duration.
- Retailers also serve as an important interface for communication with end user: They convey their opinion of product to

the end users and also form a conduit for communication of feedback from end users to the company.

Every tier added to the distribution should be justified in terms of cost incurred for their services, and such inputs are considered while developing the distribution design.

19

Are Distributors Still Relevant?

With the strides made in logistics and banking, the role of the distributor must be redefined. Each product will require some support in its journey to the final consumer. How can this movement from the manufacturer to the consumer be shortened?

Distributors, as mentioned earlier, represent the company in the markets assigned to them. They form the conduit for flow of products from company to subsequent intermediaries in the distribution chain. They are the interface between the company and the rest of the intermediaries such as wholesalers and retailers.

This role of being a conduit for the flow of goods, and also the role of being an interface with the retailer and wholesaler, is necessary as it becomes unmanageable for the company to sell directly to the large number of wholesalers and even larger number of retailers, managing inventory, stock movement and payments. The distributor, therefore becomes a necessity in the distribution chain.

However, with significant advancements in technology related to logistics and payments, several new methods of distribution could be explored in a manner that will reduce the cost of operations.

Distributors are appointed to cover a larger geographic area, and, with the support of technology, they are able to manage business dealings with a significantly larger number of retailers.

Similarly, with the change from the differential state-wise tax to the GST method of taxation, the need for state-wise warehousing no longer exists. This results in fewer warehouses with each warehouse managing the needs of a much larger number of sales points. Modern warehouse management techniques are used to manage the resultant large volume of stocks and high frequency of receipts and dispatches.

With advancements in technology, some of the changes that are being explored are as follows:

- Fewer number of warehouses across the country, resulting in far fewer stocking points of inventory.

- Fewer, larger and more modernized warehouses improve costs efficiencies in the entire storage and transportation activity
- Fewer and larger distributors covering a much larger number of retailers spread across a larger geographical area.
- Increased share of direct sales from distributors to retailers is possible due technology by monitoring inventory levels at every retail and arranging for refill sales in the most efficient manner. This reduces, if not eliminates, the role of a wholesaler.
- Payment from retailers can be managed with the advanced payment systems such that market credit can be managed within the accepted norms.
- For product categories that require fewer number of final selling points, elimination of distributors through adoption of direct shipments from warehouse to final retailer can also be considered.
- GPS used for tracking of movement goods on real-time basis facilitates inventory control besides timely deliveries.

Essentially, the focus shifts from sales push to generating the required sales pull in the market. The sales team manages the product refill at various points in the distribution chain in the most cost-effective manner, demand generation being addressed by the marketing team with their own competencies in the area.

20

What Is the Area of Coverage Planned?

Startup needs to define whether the availability of product will be pan-India or regional and then determine density of coverage required in every market selected.

The startup, when reaching the go-to market stage, would need to take a major decision on defining the geographic area of the market it proposes to target. This decision would have significant implications on many other aspects of the distribution besides determining the manning levels required to handle the sales function.

A few major issues to be addressed while determining the geographic area of the target market are as follows:

- Need to assess the financial resources available for the startup to support the operations at pan-India level, regional level or town level.
- In a phased-out launch, one needs to consider the risk of entry by me-too products, especially when the product being launched is innovative and new to the market.
- Need to assess the manufacturing capacity to support the launch at pan-India level; the question to be answered is 'Will the business run the risk of short supply after having invested in creation of demand?'
- Has test market been done on small scale in actual market conditions to ensure that the possible deficiencies in product or process have been removed before taking on the pan-India launch?
- Ability to hire and train the required number of sales team personnel to operate in the various markets that have been selected needs to be assessed.
- If pan-India launch has been decided, then the next decision is the sequence of launch and the period over which the product will be launched in various states.
- The possibilities of media support for a pan-India launch or even regional launch and the cost efficiencies of the same.

After reviewing the above issues, the point that needs to be considered at the next level is the expected volume from each of the geographical areas selected for the launch. Several issues that could be addressed to help this decision of launch are listed below:

- Who is the target consumer for the product you propose to sell? What is his demographic profile?
- What is the share of the population that meets the identified demographic profile in the markets selected for launch?
- What is the per capita consumption of the product category that you are involved with and what is the share of the market that you propose to acquire?
- Answers to the above questions would provide indicative volumes that could be expected to be achieved from the selected market.
- What is the frequency of consumption of the product? This has implications on frequency of refill required to be achieved by the distribution chain.
- What is the shelf life of the product? Does it affect the refilling cycle required for the product?

Another critical aspect to be considered is the outlet placement levels.

- What is the population of retail outlets that stock the product category in the markets selected for launch?
- What is the share of these outlets that you will aim for stocking of your products?
- The above two will indicate the number of outlets that require to be covered by the sales team or the distribution network.
- The frequency of such coverage would also be determined by the nature of product and competitive pressures, besides cost estimate for coverage of market.

- Answers to the above questions will indicate the number of feet on street to be engaged to deliver the expected share of outlets stocking your product, hence the manning levels of the sales team in the market selected for launch.
- It will also indicate the number of distributors that may be required to reach these outlets at the desired frequency of refill.

The above questions highlight the issues that need to be addressed while determining the intensity of coverage in the markets selected and the resultant manning levels that would be required to take charge of the sales operations in the area.

21

What Should Be the Trade Margin?

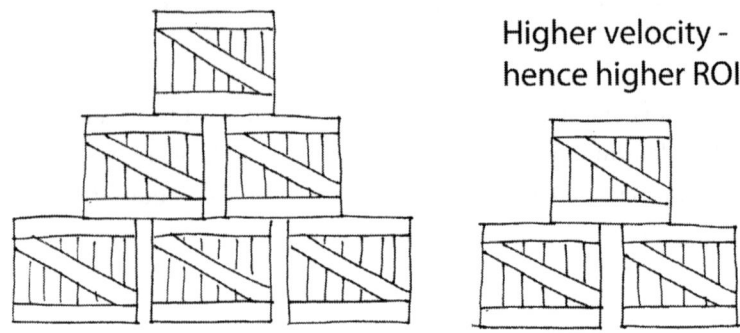

Higher velocity -
hence higher ROI

What is the correct way to arrive at the margin? Higher the velocity lower could be the margin.

In the process of transit of goods from the supplier or manufacturer to the final stage, when it is picked up by the end user, goods get handled by various intermediaries in the distribution chain. The nature of the intermediary and the number of intermediaries depends on the distribution design adopted for the given product and the prevailing market practices in the industry if relevant.

The margins earned by each of these intermediaries to perform their respective role in the distribution design for the product is known as the trade margin (TM).

Let us take the example of one of the intermediaries to get an understanding of the concept of gross margin (GM), TM, profit percentage, velocity of money (VM) and return on investment (ROI).

Intermediary: Distributor

This intermediary, being the sole representative of the company in the assigned area, needs to operate as per company guidelines in terms of pricing. The earnings are dependent on the pricing specified by the company which covers the purchase price of products and the recommended selling price. The difference between the selling price and the purchase price of the product is the GM earned by the distributor. This GM is expected to cover the operating cost of the business, and the amount left over is termed as net margin or TM.

In order to improve the TM, the business would either have to increase the turnover and/or reduce the operating costs.

Parameters Relevant in the Calculation of Margins

- Monthly sales value (MSV)
- Purchase cost of goods sold (COG)
- Monthly operating costs (MOC)

  - Office rental
  - Warehouse cost
  - Salary cost of personnel assigned to the business
  - Incentives for personnel assigned to the business
  - Distribution costs—transportation, van hire cost, fuel, etc.
  - Electricity
  - Taxes

- Money invested (MI) in the business

  - MI to hold required inventory level at all times
  - Credit in the market (average credit value)
  - Receivables from company towards claims for schemes/ product replacements, etc.
  - Other one-time investments towards acquiring building, infrastructure, vehicles, etc.

Profit Margin Calculations Using above Parameters

- $GM = MSV - COG$
  GM is the money earned monthly after deducting COG from MSV

- Net margin or $TM = GM - MOC$
  TM is the money earned monthly after deducting MOC from GM

- PM = TM/MI in percentage

  PM is monthly TM earned divided by MI in the business, expressed as percentage

- VM = MSV/MI

  VM is the number of times MI in the business is turned over in a month. When MSV is divided by MI in the business, it gives a factor that represents the number of times MI is turned over in a month.

- ROI = PM × VM × 12 months in percentage

  ROI indicates the return earned for MI in the business, which is expressed in percentage per annum. To arrive at this number, PM percentage is multiplied by VM and 12 (representing 12 months).

  For example, if PM of a distributor is 2 per cent and VM is 1.5, then ROI is (2 × 1.5 × 12) 36 per cent.

  ROI is a good comparative measure to assess whether it was worthwhile to have invested in the business compared to alternate areas of investment such as banks or other business opportunities

Concept of Profit Margin

It is clear from the above that higher the MSV, higher will be the GM earned every month and higher will be the TM earned every month. This happens only because some of the costs such as office rental, warehouse costs, salary of sales personnel, electricity, etc., does not increase with increase in turnover. So such fixed costs get covered by higher GM earned due to higher turnover and hence results in higher TM. Higher the TM earned on the MI, higher will be the PM.

So, the ways to increase PM is to either increase MSV or reduce MOC.

Concept of Velocity of Money

Velocity of money (VM) represents the number of times the MI is turned around in a month. For a given level of investment (MI), the higher MSV, the higher would be the VM.

If MSV divided by MI is equal to 1 then VM = 1
If MSV divided by MI is equal to 2 then VM = 2

To improve the returns on the investments made in a business, we need to make efforts to increase the VM. This can be done by either increasing the turnover (MSV) at a given level of investment (MI) or decreasing the level of investment (MI) without lowering the turnover (MSV).

Concept of Return on Investment

ROI = PM × VM × 12 months (in percentage)

The two factors that determine the ROI are the PM and the VM. Higher the PM or higher the VM, greater will be the ROI. So even if PM is low, efforts could be made to increase VM, then the ROI will increase significantly. If, for example, PM is 2 per cent and VM is 1 then

ROI = 2 × 1 × 12 months = 24%

If PM is 2 per cent and VM is 1.5 then

ROI = 2 × 1.5 × 12 months = 36%

Therefore, distributors would aim at reducing inventory levels, reduce credit in market, etc., to achieve higher ROI.

Companies, on the other hand, would focus on an increasing turnover and thereby increase the GM earned by the distributors every month that would enable distributors to earn better ROI.

Other Intermediaries

The same principle operates at other intermediaries as well. The wholesaler, for instance, improves his turnover to the maximum level every month by retaining the lowest PM and making his products most competitively priced without increasing his inventory level or any other costs. As a result of higher VM, they earn very high ROI.

22

What Should Be the Trade Payment Terms?

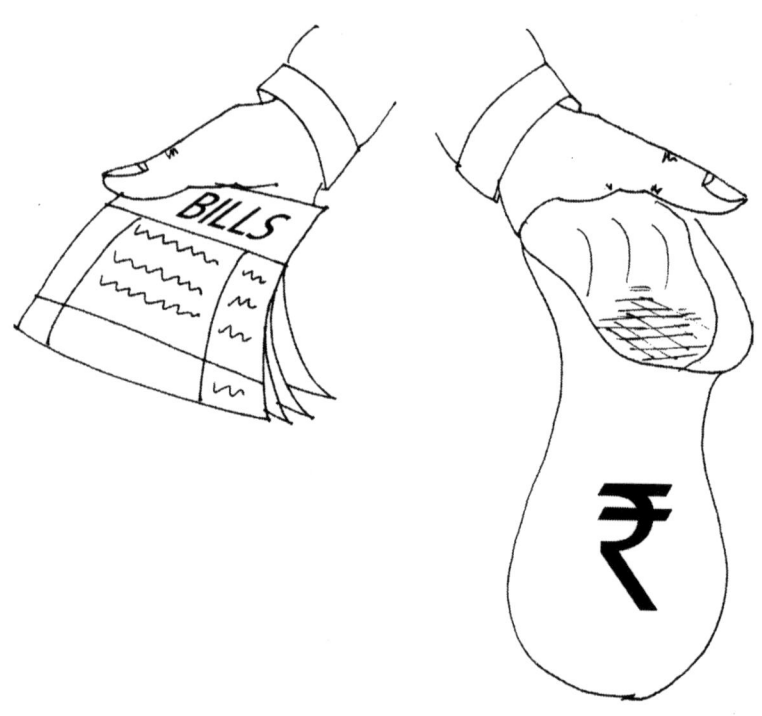

The management of credit is a critical function which determines the success of your business. When badly handled, sales teams end up chasing payments rather than orders. How should credit be handled?

Credit is the basis on which any business operates; yet, it is the basis on which many businesses fail if not managed properly.

The ideal situation is when the credit is neither offered to buyers nor is it taken from suppliers—in other words, it's a cash deal through the entire distribution chain. But this never happens in reality.

In a buyer–seller relationship, it's the buyer who asks for credit and it is for the seller to accept this demand or reject the same and insist on advance payment or payment on delivery. This decision to accept or reject such a request is based on several factors; some of these are listed here:

- How critical is the business from the specific buyer?
- How strong is your competitive position in the market?
- What is your capability to service high frequency refills for the buyer?
- What is the credit worthiness of the buyer?
- What is the general practice in the market in the relevant product category?

Another perspective to view the credit, especially for new entrants in the business, is to view the entire credit being given for a specific quantity of product as simply a case of shifting the product from your warehouse to customers shelf. Inventory maintained in the customers shelf surely has higher chance of being sold compared to inventory stacked in your own warehouse. So, you may like to treat it as market development expense.

Once you make the assessment and come to a conclusion that it is necessary for you to offer credit, then you need to make the terms of payment absolutely clear to the buyer detailing the value of credit, period of credit and the penal interest for delayed payment or incentive for payment on time.

The next concern area is how to ensure payment on time: It's here where advancements in technology have made it possible to get an assured payment from the customer in terms of value and time by scheduling electronic transfers. The buyer only has to make sure that adequate funds are available in the designated account and no other steps are required to be taken. The transfer of funds gets triggered on the specified date and time.

In situations where adoption of such technology for payments is not feasible, there is a need to establish accountability for collection of payments on time and a tracking system to monitor outstanding.

The genesis of delayed payments, if identified, will help implement suitable corrective measures.

Delayed Payments: A Few Causative Factors

- The seller has sold more than what the buyer actually wants at a given point in time, resulting in buyer holding unsold inventory. As long as there is unsold inventory, which is more than the norm, the buyer feels justified in delaying the payment beyond the agreed-upon schedule date.

  - Corrective action: Understand customers' needs and sell accordingly, avoid over selling.

- Unexpected downturn in demand causes slowdown in sales. This results in the buyer taking much longer time to liquidate inventory than what was assumed earlier.

  - Check trends in market of other customers and reconfirm claim of slowdown in sales; if found to be correct, then offer special one-time extension.

- Error in invoicing resulting in product categories invoiced being at variance from the order.

  - Identify source of error: Is its unclear transmission of order done by salesperson?
  - Is its unclear absence of confirmation from the customer prior to order being sent to office?
  - Take corrective action and offer one-time credit to ease problem at customer's end.

These are some of the typical triggers for delayed payments. The recommendation is to identify the source of the problem and take corrective action to prevent recurrence of the problem.

Role of Credit

Company to distributor:

- There are two specific categories of companies: one that does not give credit at all and the other that gives credit for varying periods of time depending on the needs of the situation.
- Among those who do not give credit at all, some companies insist on advance payment, others insist on cash on delivery, both of which represent nil credit.

- Since company-to-dealer sales is essentially refill sales, adoption of technology-driven payment systems triggered by inventory-level norms is observed in many cases.

Distributor to retailer:

- As distributors are located in the local market, retailers almost consider it their birthright to ask for credit. Distributors also find it convenient to accept demand for credit as it helps them to push the products of their choice into the retail shop in a manner that would block competitive products being stocked by retailer.
- Credit is used here to gain competitive edge in the marketplace.

Distributor to wholesaler:

- Credit is often given to wholesalers but the period is far less than what is offered to a retailer.
- Credit offered to a wholesaler is used a negotiating factor that helps you stock the desired quantity of your products in the wholesaler shop. This has a cascading effect in the wholesaler giving the desired support for your product in preference to competition products.
- Credit is used here to gain competitive edge.

Retailer to consumer:

- This is very dependent on the nature of the product and market.
- Some retailers offer few premium customers the facility of operating an individual account with the retailer in which all transactions are posted and the account cleared at the end of the month.

- Sometimes a premium customer is offered EMI facility so that they can spread their payment over a period of time instead of one-time payment. Several credit cards offer this facility too.

Credit, as mentioned, is an important factor of success in business. The manner in which one effectively manages credit will determine whether credit will be a boon or bane for the business.

Section VI

Time and Territory Management

The efficient use of a salesperson's time is extremely important for success. Territory management is a science that must be respected. Is it important to see every customer every month? How is the time of the salesperson utilized on a working day?

23

What Is the Concept of a Territory That Is Allotted to the Salesperson?

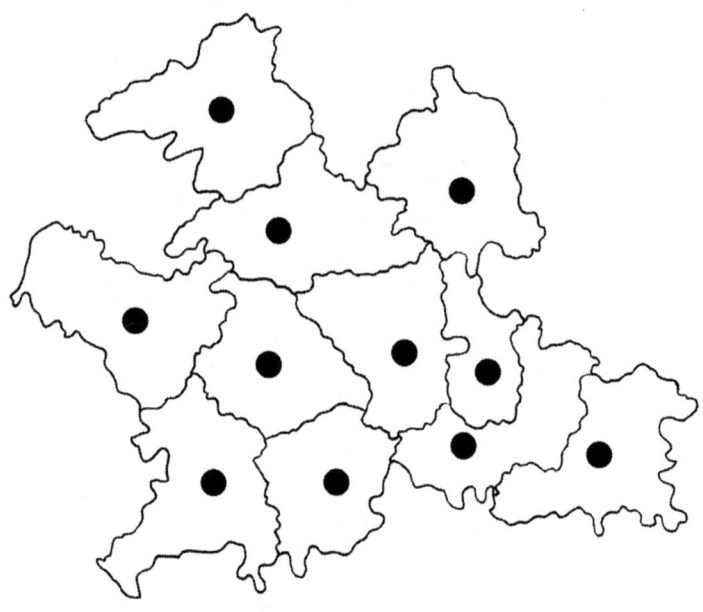

● Represents customers located in the district towns

How much is too much and how much is too little in designing a territory? Which is the territory where the salesperson spends most of the day commuting or meeting a customer? Which is the well-planned territory that utilizes salespersons resource in the most efficient manner?

An attempt to answer this question—how much is too much and how much is too little—in the designing of a territory would necessarily have to start with a need to understand what is meant by a territory.

Sales Territory

A territory is defined as a geographic area of the market that is expected to be under the charge of one frontline salesperson.

Most often, such a geographic area comprises of contiguous markets or districts or states, as this helps in ensuring that the salesperson's time is well utilized without the need for traversing markets that do not come under his charge.

However, occasions do arise to consider markets that are spread across various non-contiguous geographic areas and yet have a rationale for being clubbed under one territory. A good example would be a salesperson of Modern Format stores: He could be in charge of a number of such stores spread across cities but will not be in charge of the small retail stores market which are located in the same area.

Having explained the essential concepts and the geographic structure of a territory, we need to touch upon the important parameters that are taken into account before firming up the actual boundaries of the territory.

Parameters to Be Considered While Forming a Territory

- Need to assess the market potential of the proposed territory and compare it with the turnover that is expected to be handled by an average frontline salesperson.
- All frontline salespersons, of a similar management level, to be accountable for similar turnover or a comparable competitive market condition.
- Competitive nature of the market, besides other factors, to be assessed to determine the intensity of the coverage of the market by the salesperson.
- Geographic size of the territory is a factor that is evaluated by the physical ability of the salesperson to cover the territory at the desired frequency. Distances covered along with the time taken for travel by the salesperson often cut short the effective working hours in the market. We need to minimize travel time and maximize market-working time to improve utilization of the salesperson. Excessive commuting between markets can be physically exhausting, adversely affecting the quality of the market work.
- Transport facilities between two points of travel as well as night-halt facilities wherever and whenever required to be also taken into consideration in finalizing the territory boundary.
- Need to align the proposed territory with the census zones, states and districts. This helps to access various demographic data which will be extremely useful to determine market potential and assist in various operational decisions.

Give a Territory an ID

Once having finalized the boundaries of territory, it is given a code or a number for identification. This is incorporated into the records of the company along with the rationale and various parameters that were used to define the territory. As far as possible, territories once defined do not undergo frequent revisions. If at all changes are required to be made in the territory boundary that has already been defined, then the parameters that were used in the past would require to be revisited and changes justified before incorporating in the records of the company.

Territory Sanctity

In other words, once a territory is defined, it gains a sort of permanence. Sales personnel may resign or get re-assigned, but the territory boundaries remain the same.

If sales personnel resign or go on leaves, then the salesperson of the adjoining territory (or any other salesperson) takes additional charge of such a territory that has been vacated until a replacement salesperson is found to handle the territory.

A well-planned territory is a great help in the efficient working of a sales team. A sales job is fraught with facing the elements of weather, transport delays and cumulative fatigue. Salespersons need to face the market every morning having rested well the previous night and be on time to make a difference to the efforts in establishing the startup brand.

24

What Is a Planned Journey Cycle?

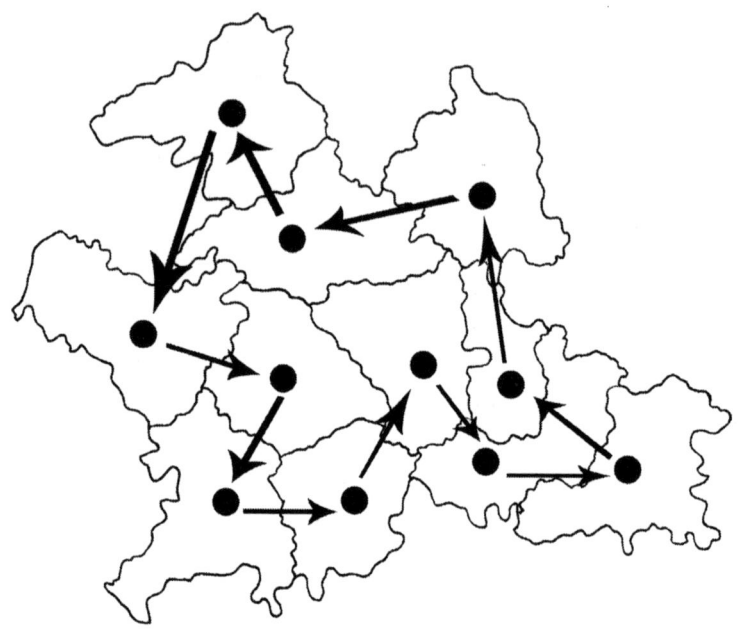

Route map with the least backtracking

WHAT IS A PLANNED JOURNEY CYCLE?

A planned journey cycle (PJC) is an attempt to cover a territory in a judicious pattern. Is it applicable to a new product line? Or can we just take each day as it comes and make the best of it?

Having got an understanding of what is meant by the term 'territory' in the sales arena, we are aware that frontline salesperson assigned to be in charge of the territory is the company resource responsible for maximizing sales in the area. This salesperson brings with him his knowledge of the market and selling skills acquired over the years of experience. A critical input to maximize the utilization of his knowledge and skills is the manner in which he manages his time. It is here we apply the concept of PJC.

Inputs to be considered while developing a PJC for the salesperson assigned to a given territory are as follows:

- Geographic boundary and a map of the territory.
- Location of dealers, stockists, retailers in various towns of the territory.
- Desired frequency of visit to the dealers, stockists and retailers within the territory.
- Transport modes available to reach the desired markets of the territory and the expenses incurred.
- Availability of night-halt facility in various towns and the expenses incurred.
- Number of days required to be at office for planning, attending meetings, training, coordinating activities and follow up in a month.
- Number of working days expected to be clocked in a month/ year.
- Would the repetitive cycle of PJC be based on calendar month or four weeks? If former, then the year will have 12 PJCs, but, if the latter, the year will have 13 PJCs.

All the inputs listed above follow a simple guideline: What are the activities expected to be accomplished and what is the time available? There are a set of activities that are specifically devoted to selling and the rest of the activities are support related. While designing a PJC, the objective would be to maximize the amount of time available for market work and allocate the least amount of time that is required to fulfil the needs of the support activities.

Given below is an example of the PJC developed on the basis of a four-week cycle. You will observe that there are separate allocations of time to market working days and meetings or office days.

PJC based on the four-week cycle
(4 weeks × 13 cycles = 52 weeks)

Week level

- Working days/week: 6-day week (Monday to Saturday)

Journey cycle (JC) level

- JC: 4 weeks per JC
- Working days per JC: 4 weeks × 6 days = 24 days per JC
- Review/planning meetings per JC: 2 day per JC. Such meetings held on second and fourth Saturdays of the JC
- Market days per JC: 24 − 2 = 22 days

Annual level

- JC per year: 13 JC
- Weeks per JC × No of JC per year = 4 × 13 = 52 weeks
- Working days per year: 13 × 24 = 312 days

- Market days per year: 13 × 22 = 286 days
- Meeting days per year: 13 × 2 = 26 days

Having determined the minimum days that are required to be spent in the market as explained above, effort is to be made to design the travel schedule covering various markets in a manner it minimizes time spent in travel and maximizes time spent in the market engaged in actual sales activity. In the example above, if 22 days have been allocated to market work over the four-week period, the spread will be as follows:

- First week: 6 days market work
- Second week: 5 days market work, followed by 1 day in office
- Third week: 6 days market work
- Fourth week: 5 days market work, followed by 1 day in office

While designing the travel schedule to cover the market as per the above plan, we need to take into consideration the parameters listed above and ensure that time spent by salesperson in actual selling is maximized.

25

Does Pareto Apply in Territory Management?

A

B

B

B

The principle of equity rather than equality defines allocation of resources when a product is launched. It is necessary to allocate more time to high potential customers rather than giving equal time to all customers.

When time is a constraint, there is a need to utilize this valuable resource in a manner that produces the maximum efficiency in work. The skill of planning one's time enables one to be more productive than the one who does not utilize time in a well-planned manner.

The Pareto Principle, named after its founder, the Italian economist Vilfredo Pareto, who first wrote about it in 1895, is one of the most useful concepts in time management. It is popularly known as the 80/20 rule or the law of the vital few. It is based on the finding that 80 per cent of the effect comes from 20 per cent of the causes. In the sales arena, there are several decisions where this 80/20 principle is widely used.

When one reviews the distributor-wise sales of a territory, it will be often observed that 20 per cent of the distributors would account for 80 per cent of the total sales of the territory, clearly establishing the case of the law of the vital few. As the salesperson needs to ensure that his time is well utilized, it will not be advisable for him to spend equal amount of time with all his distributors regardless of the value of business generated by them. It would be important for him to allocate a higher share of this time with the 20 per cent of the distributors that account for 80 per cent of the sales of his territory.

Typical Example of Use of 80/20 Principle in Sales Arena

- Draw up a full list of distributors in the territory along with their annual sales value.
- Arrange the list in the decreasing order of sales value.

- Express the share of each distributor in terms of percentage of total sales value of territory.
- Draw up the cumulative share of total sales value.
- Distributors that account for 80 per cent of the total territory sales value are identified.
- It would be observed that the top 20 per cent of the distributors account for close to 80 per cent of total territory sales value.
- Classify these select distributors as major and the rest of the distributors in the territory as minor.

A working example of the above steps has been tabulated in Annexure 1. This table explains the adoption of the 80/20 principle in the classification of distributors into major and minor. Such classification is useful in the allocation of resources—financial and material—and even time management of sales personnel.

A common example of use of such a principle is the allocation of a market-development budget across the country or allocation of market working days when developing the PJC of the sales personnel. (For tabulation details, refer to Annexure 1.)

26

How Can a Salesperson Develop Sales?

The major role of a salesperson launching a new product must be the activity that would generate awareness and interest for the product. Orders booked must be a function of the developmental activities conducted in the territory.

Sales personnel often believe that their sole responsibility is to sell and hence rarely consider generating demand as part of their role. This limited view of their responsibility could have emerged due to the fact that efforts in the direction of demand-generation activity does not produce immediate visible results and hence does not give them the much-wanted adrenalin. This belief tends to make sales personnel focus on customers who are their regular buyers of existing products and expect them to buy the new product being launched by their company. This tendency limits the market exposure for the new product and hence the market potential and consequently has an adverse impact on the future of the new product.

Every frontline salesperson should believe that he is the owner of the business and should constantly think of growing the business with a long-term perspective in the most efficient manner. He may not have the skills to design activities that trigger demand for sales of the new product—a role which is normally handled by the product promotion team or the marketing department. However, he has to recognize the importance of implementing such market development activities that have been designed by the marketing team or the product promotion team and ensure its effective implementation as per expected schedule as this ensures long-term success of the new product in the territory assigned to him/her.

A Case of a New Variant of Milk Being Launched by a Successful Dairy Firm

A typical example of a new product launch is when a successful dairy firm engaged in the business of supplying fresh dairy milk daily to a large number of customers in a country over several years develops a new variant of the fresh milk which is healthier for the customer but priced marginally higher. The success of this new variant is critical for the company as it generates a higher PM.

The marketing team did a good job of designing launch campaigns for the product using media and ground-level promotional activities. While there was hardly any involvement of the sales personnel in the success of the media campaign, the market-level promotional activities were entirely dependent on the active participation of the field sales personnel. It's at this juncture that the sales personnel had to make a difficult choice—do I spend time on market development activities to promote the new variant of milk whose sales volume at the present is hardly exciting or do I put in a bit more effort to get higher sales from my regular range of products and achieve my targets.

It's here that effective leadership plays a significant role. An effective leader spends time with his frontline sales team to share the company perspective of how important it is for the company to succeed in the new variant of milk and ensure that total market share of the company reaches the desired level. He must explain the important role played by the current frontline sales personnel in implementing ground-level promotional campaigns for the new variant to help achieve increased awareness and high levels of trial and repeat buys. Such high level of involvement by the leadership is a must for success.

The differential performance of teams that adopt this approach would make sales personnel recognize the cardinal truth in sales: 'Orders booked today is a function of the developmental activities conducted in the market yesterday.'

Emerging from the above understanding, the sales personnel would require to incorporate such developmental activities as part of their regular PJC planning in the respective territory.

Section VII

Reporting by Sales Team

Salespeople universally dislike reporting. It is considered an unnecessary waste of time. Often there is a feeling that no one reads the reports anyway. The principle of reporting has definite effect on the performance of the sales team. It must be insisted upon.

27

What Are the Types of Reports Submitted by the Sales Team?

Just about, everybody reports sales orders, but it is more important to understand the development activities conducted by the sales team. Building a brand becomes the major responsibility of the sales team.

Sales function is primarily a team effort, and it is common knowledge that for a team to succeed there is a need for excellent communication between members of the team as well as between members and the leader of the team. Criticality of such communication is more than evident in team games.

When a salesperson is assigned a role in the field, he is invariably focused on outcomes or deliverables, which is sales orders obtained. While reporting of outcomes is important, it's equally important to report details of inputs or efforts to achieve the desired outcomes. This is because the efficiency of implementing the inputs or activities has a major role in determining the outcomes.

The working of the sales team personnel is designed in such a manner that his total working day is utilized in the most efficient manner; as discussed earlier, such a design would operate on the guideline of minimizing time spent on support activities and maximizing time spent on actual sales activities. If the salesperson is expected to clock 22 market days per PJC, there is a need for him to report his actual number of market days in a periodic manner so that both, he and his supervisor, are able to take immediate corrective action, if at all there are shortfalls compared to expected levels of market days. A similar tracking of number of customers visited in a day is essential; hence, reporting of customer visits per day is an essential parameter in the reporting system.

Similar is the need to keep track of the market development activities that are expected to be completed by the salesperson in a given timeframe: Typical market development activities could be roadshows or demos held in the market, customer awareness programmes conducted, house-to-house campaigns conducted, number of sign boards put up at key vantage points to aid in building brand awareness, etc. All such market development activities are expected to be completed by sales personnel in a given timeframe, say within a PJC. Such development activities may not result in immediate outcomes but surely play a significant role in influencing outcomes or sales in the period ahead. A salesperson is a key person in the implementation of such development activities and hence performance of such development activities needs tracking compared to plan.

The wide range of reporting parameters can be broadly classified into three groups.

Group 1

This relates to recording the details of days worked by salesperson compared to an expected level during a given timeframe such as PJC or a month, quarter or year.

A few examples of such parameters reported are as follows:

- Working days
- Market days
- Meeting days
- Sick leave days
- Casual leave days
- Holidays

Group 2

This set relates to parameters that record the different activities that are to be completed in the course of a market day; these are as follows:

- Customers visited per market day
- New customers visited per market day

- Worked alone in the market
- Worked with superior in the market
- Worked with others in the market
- Defined development activities completed in PJC

Parameters listed in both the groups, 1 and 2, are related to the input provided to achieve the desired outcome. There is an expected level or norm for this range of inputs to be given by the salesperson in the marketplace. Reporting of the actual inputs given by the salesperson in defined timeframe, be it PJC, month, quarter or year, forms the main focus of such periodic reporting. These parameters do vary from industry to industry, but the essential principle remains the same across industries.

Group 3

This group focuses on parameters that are related to the outcomes. Salesperson would be expected to achieve a given level of outcomes, be it sales volume, sales value or profitability or cost issues. There is a need for close monitoring of actual outcomes in comparison to the outcomes expected to be achieved by the salesperson in a given timeframe. A list of typical parameters considered in this group is as follows (these vary across industries):

- Sales volume until date for the PJC in progress
- Sales value until date for the PJC in progress
- Average sales value per unit
- Selling cost per unit of sale
- Distribution cost per unit of sale
- GM per unit of sales
- Average sale value per customer
- Average productive calls per day

- Average sale value per productive call
- Value of outstanding at end of previous PJC

The above forms only a typical list. The actual parameters would vary from industry to industry.

28

What Are the Principles Adopted for Reporting?

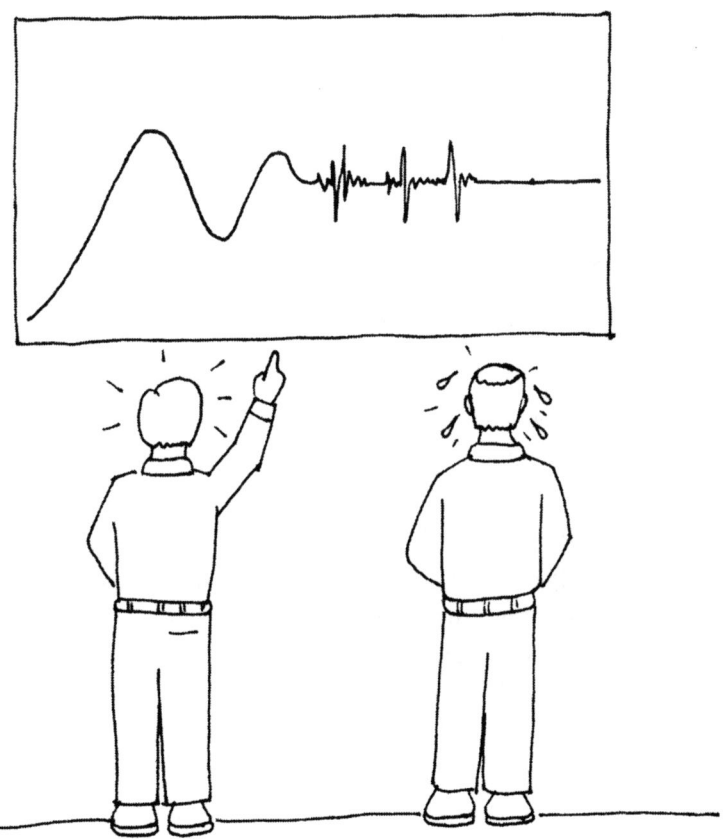

Timely reporting is an important aspect of monitoring strategic plan. Often, it takes time for the information to get back on whether a strategy is working or not. Modification of strategy is called for to ensure that goals are met. Succinct reporting with a provision for feedback is imperative.

Sales reporting is considered by most sales personnel to be one of the most disliked aspects of the job. The reason for such an opinion can be often attributed to not knowing the purpose of reporting. Therefore, it is useful to understand the purpose of sales reporting and the principles adopted for reporting.

The two broad objectives of sales reporting are discussed in brief here.

Salesperson: Feedback for Own Corrective Action

- Sales report provides the person an opportunity to observe areas of shortfall compared to expected levels of performance and trains the mind to focus on those areas and take mid-course corrective action. For instance, if report of the day worked indicates that the salesperson has achieved less than the expected average value per call, this parameter will be flagged for his own attention while working in the market on the following day. This enables performance improvement without the need for corrective action by supervisor.
- It provides the salesperson an opportunity to step back a bit and recognize what has been achieved by him in the stated timeframe. Unless this opportunity is provided, the salesperson will tend to get lost in the details and not get an overall broad perspective of how his territory is performing.
- It enables the salesperson get an assessment of the weak spots in the territory and in turn aid in the development of a growth plan through in-depth market-wise knowledge.

- It serves as a reference material on work done during the previous visit to the customer so that one can be far better prepared to conduct the discussion effectively with the customer in the subsequent visit.

Sales Manager: Feedback on Performance of Members of the Team

- Reporting from members of the team enables the manager to get a quick assessment of progress in the implementation of the plan agreed upon and take midcourse corrective action wherever required.
- It provides an effective tool to evaluate the performance of different members of his team in a periodic manner which helps in coaching and counselling them to improve their respective performance.
- It provides inputs for reporting on the status of performance of his entire region to the superior at the regional or national level.
- It also provides market-level feedback on performance of competition, a very important feedback for the top management.

Principles of Reporting

Design of reports:

- Design should be standardized for all reports on a given topic across geographic regions to enable aggregation at various levels of management.
- The identity of sender and receiver to be assigned to one specific area of the report for ease of reference.

- The details of period of reference to be assigned to one specific area of the report for ease of reference.
- Provisions to be made for writer to incorporate his comments and signature at the bottom so that he ensures he reviews his own report before it is submitted.
- Care to be taken to minimize repetitive written work, therefore contents of report to be system generated as far as possible.

Practice of reporting:

- Time spent by salesperson writing the report should be minimal, but time spent by salesperson reviewing the report written should not be limited.
- Salesperson to ensure that the frequency of report be maintained as prescribed and not aggregated over a period to be sent in one lot. For instance, daily report needs to be submitted daily and not aggregated to be sent on weekly basis.
- The sales manager should demonstrate evidence of having read the reports sent by his team members by highlighting specific inputs and commending his efforts or guiding her/him to take corrective action to achieve improved performance levels.
- The sales manager should use the contents of reports submitted by his team members at the periodic review sessions so that feedback is data based as well as it conveys the importance of good quality report writing by salesperson.

As the organization expands its operations, the importance of good quality and timely report writing increases as it becomes impossible for senior management to be present in several places at the same time. Reports are the only source for senior management to be kept updated and to be able to take corrective action on the strategies that have been implemented. It is the high quality and timely reporting by members of the sales team that ensures management decisions are correct.

29

Typical Sales Reporting Topics and Formats

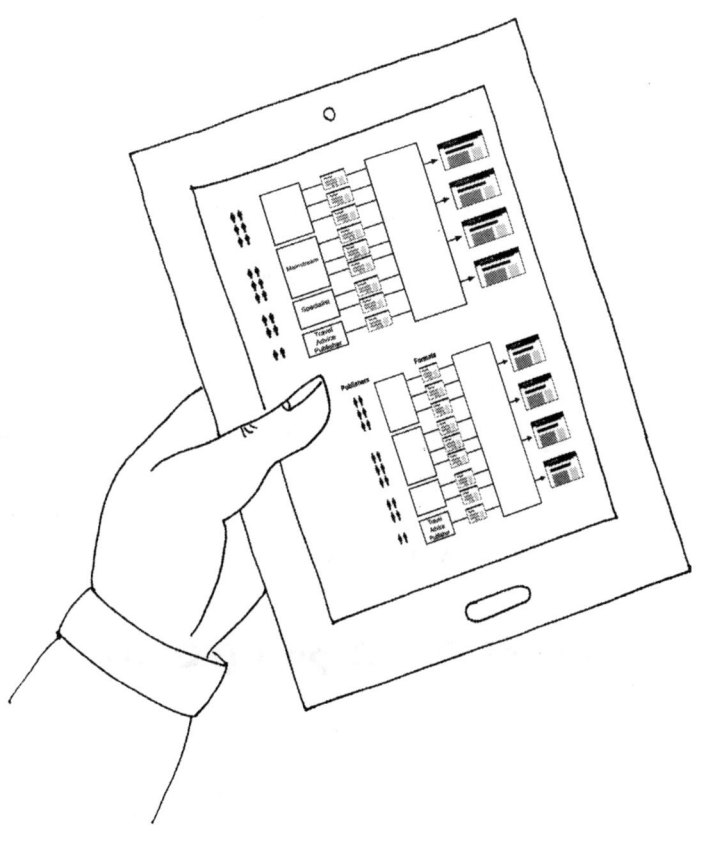

In this chapter, some examples of formats aspects of reporting will be dealt with in some detail.

Every company has its own range of reports that are designed to meet the needs of the organization keeping in mind the specific characteristics of the industry they participate in. While they differ from industry to industry, the essential features remain the same. We shall, in the next few pages, deal with some of the most common reports indicating the typical formats adopted and also state the basic objective of these reports.

Daily Market Report (DMR)

DMR of a typical frontline salesperson reports the details of the day's activities and outcomes which is necessary to be sent to his reporting manager on daily basis.

This report provides a summary of what has been done during the day in the market and what has been achieved in terms of activity and outcome. It's a very critical report that informs the superior on the working of his subordinates in their respective territories. (Sample of report is provided in Annexure 2.)

Frequency of Visit Report (FOVR)

FOVR is a summary report of the working of the sales personnel in terms of distributors visited and dates of visits and hence frequency of visit. This is one sheet maintained for all the 13 JCs, which provides an overview of the working of the sales personnel for the whole year. The categorization of distributor into major/minor gives a guideline on the expected frequency of visit to the distributor(s) and the actual frequency, which could be compared to assess whether actual is as per expected norm. (Sample of report is provided in Annexure 3.)

Distributor Visit Report (DVR)

DVR reflects all the details that have been discussed during the visit to the distributor(s). DVR provides data for reference, the annual sales of distributor in the preceding year as well as the corresponding average per JC. It also provides a reference to the past performance levels of distributor in term of sales until date or year-to-date sales (normally called YTD). This enables comparison of current performance level on all these parameters with the past performance levels and take corrective action wherever necessary.

A section is provided to state in brief the topics discussed, action taken and action to be taken. This is an excellent reference to be looked up prior to the next visit to the distributor(s) besides serving as an immediate reminder for action to be taken.

There is a section which provides a checklist of points, which is normally expected to be touched upon by the salesperson during the visit to the distributor.

The next section covers the retail points that have been visited in the markets covered by distributor. This section provides a brief glimpse of competition present at retail points and how one's own brand is positioned in the relevant industry.

The last section provides the final outcome of the visit in terms of orders booked, agreed-upon delivery terms and price. It also provides space for orders discussed and confirmation awaited.

At the bottom left corner, there is a small section which provides a quick reference to the manner in which the market was covered— whether covered alone or with superior or with others from the company. It indicates whether the date of visit to the market is as per date planned in the PJC. The report ends with the signature of the writer and provides space for the signature of the superior.

DVR's main advantage is that it reminds the sales personnel of the actions to be taken soon after the visit as well as provides a quick reference point to be looked up prior to the next visit to the distributor. Every visit to the distributor will have a new DVR, all of which will be filed in the space allocated for a given distributor. (Sample of report is provided in Annexure 4.)

Planned Journey Cycle (PJC)

PJC report is prepared prior to the commencement of every JC. It is essentially a plan of travel that covers the distributors located in the territory as per frequency of visit desired as well as market contingencies of the JC. It lists the distributor to be visited on every single market day and covers all the days of the week. It also assigns the agreed-upon date on which sales personnel will attend meetings at the office. So, the entire work plan is developed by sales personnel and approval obtained from his superior. Thereafter the actual working progresses as per PJC are developed and approved unless there are unexpected developments that necessitate deviation from dates or markets planned in the PJC. (Sample of report is provided in Annexure 5.)

Section VIII

Costing of a Sales Team

The total cost of running a sales operation can sometimes be a shock, especially in the early months when the returns are not commensurate. It is necessary to understand the various allied costs that are part of having a sales team.

30

Elements of Cost That Are Considered in Costing of Sales Team

Often only the salary of the sales team is considered as a cost. In reality, there is an equal amount of cost that is incurred when the team operates in the market. This includes travel, transportation, hotel accommodation, food, communication and other expenses.

Beyond the capital costs or one-time costs incurred towards building, machinery and other development costs, there are recurring costs that are directly proportional to the quantum of goods produced, transported and sold. This part of the investment chain that covers expenses incurred towards raw material and/or manufacturing of goods and transportation of goods up to warehouse established in various locations is treated as basic cost of goods. For ease of understanding, we shall refer to this as pre-sales costs.

It is from this point onwards that the sales team gets involved and conducts the sales operations that enable sales of goods that have reached the warehouse. The sales team may have sales offices either located in important business centres or located as part of the warehouse facility.

There are three categories of costs incurred in this part of the investment chain:

- Expenses incurred towards the maintenance of a sales team and expenses incurred by them in the course of performing their job
- Expenses incurred towards the transportation of goods from warehouse to distributors or final selling points
- Administrative cost of managing a sales office, if any

The above three categories of costs are referred to as sales costs.

The break-even for the sales team therefore would be when revenue or net sales value covers pre-sales cost plus sales cost. In other words, all expense that the sales team incurs in the course of conducting the sales operations must be recovered in full from the sales value generated over and above the value required to meet pre-sales cost.

This critical equation ensures that all expenses incurred on sales team and related activities must be closely monitored so that there is an assurance of recovery of the money from the sales volume generated by the sales team.

Cost of sales team could be reviewed under the following broad groups and sub-groups. The items listed in each group are by no means exhaustive. Expense head would vary from industry to industry. It is always useful to compare notes with other companies dealing with competition products as well as non-competition products operating in similar geographic areas.

Cost incurred on salesperson towards earnings:

- Salary
- Incentive
- Bonus
- House rent allowance
- Leave travel allowance
- Medical allowance/reimbursement
- Provident fund
- Other allowances

Cost incurred by salesperson towards the conduct of sales activities:

- Travel expense
- Night halt expense—hotel stay
- Food allowance, while on market work
- Local transportation
- Mobile phone expenses
- Stationery expenses

Cost incurred towards logistics and infrastructure:

- Office rental
- Electricity costs
- Administrative cost
- Administrative staff salaries and incidentals
- Warehouse costs
- Transportation cost from warehouse to customer
- Telephone/Wi-Fi
- Insurance

These costs are not normally independent of the sales team cost. It covers expenditure towards support activity such as transportation, storage, office rental, insurance, utilities.

All the above are the common heads under which costs are monitored. It might vary from industry to industry and depends on the design adopted for selling of the goods.

31

Why Is It Important to Arrive at the Planned Journey Cycle Cost?

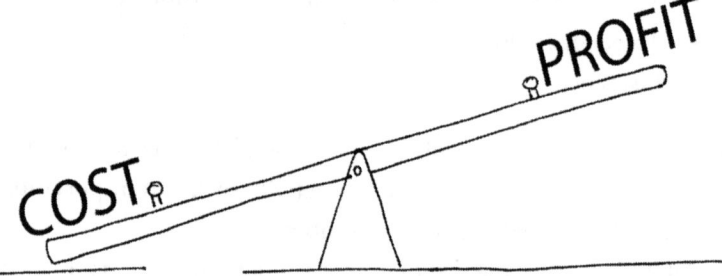

Any sales function has a break-even cost. This helps to understand the efficiency of the sales effort. For a new company, a sales team that covers its cost is a great advantage. It is building brand equity at no additional cost.

As explained in the earlier section, PJC represents the travel plan of the sales personnel in the territory assigned to him. This travel plan is either monthly in which case it is repeated 12 times a year (12 months) or a four-week cycle in which case it would be repeated 13 times a year (13×4 weeks). Regardless of the travel-plan design adopted, one important aspect to be recognized is that it is an activity focused on generating business from the specific territory and it is repeated 12 times or 13 times a year.

It therefore becomes essential to keep a close tab on the expenses planned to be incurred for conducting a PJC and measure it against the revenue planned to be generated from one PJC. While the metric is common, the percentage would vary from industry to industry.

This metric has several advantages that would help the overall cost efficiency of the sales organization. PJC cost as percentage turnover generated from the territory is a good measure to compare the cost efficiencies of different territories generating business for the company. This could help identify the less cost-efficient territories and develop specific corrective measures to reduce or eliminate the cost inefficiencies.

This metric, when less than the norm expected, gives an opportunity to review elements of PJC cost and turnover in the following manner:

- Travel cost:

  - Is travel cost high due to ineffective route planning?
  - Is travel cost high due to erroneous assessment on frequency needed to cover markets?

- Does the route plan involve back tracking and hence incurring avoidable travel costs?
- Are there lower cost options of travel possible?
- Revisit the design of the territory in terms of size and business volume expected—is there scope for improvement?

- Cost of stay:

  - Need to explore lower cost options for stay without compromising on comfort or safety.
  - Are there possibilities of reducing the number of nights spent in hotels by using overnight travel options?

- Communication cost:

  - Are there ways to reduce cost of communication? For instance, using standardized reports on email instead of talking on phone, lower cost options for mobile connection plans from service providers, etc.

- Turnover issues:

  - Is the turnover of distributors assigned to the territory adequate to justify the frequency of visit by salesperson?
  - Is the low turnover only a short-term problem? Is there a potential to increase turnover with the increased level of focus by salesperson in the medium term?
  - Is there a need for realigning the territory, as the turnover expected to be generated by the current set of distributors may not justify the attention of one salesperson?

While all the above parameters are related to reviewing the PJC cost at the planning stage, there is another aspect of PJC cost which allows one to compare actuals against plan.

A given territory at the start of the year has an approved PJC which takes into consideration the approved design of the territory and the travel plans required to generate the targeted sales volume from the territory. This is the plan based on which the salesperson manages his territory.

However, there could be many deviations from the plan depending on the manner in which the territory is managed. Greater the deviations, lesser is the efficiency (assuming that the PJC cost has been designed in the most cost-effective manner).

There could be more visits than planned. There could be backtracking of routes resulting in increased travel costs. There could be unexpected situations that call for emergency high-cost travel rather than low-cost travel options planned in the PJC.

Therefore, it's important to monitor actual JC cost compared to planned PJC cost at the end of every JC to enable to take corrective action wherever required.

32

What Is the Concept of Daily Allowance or Bhatta?

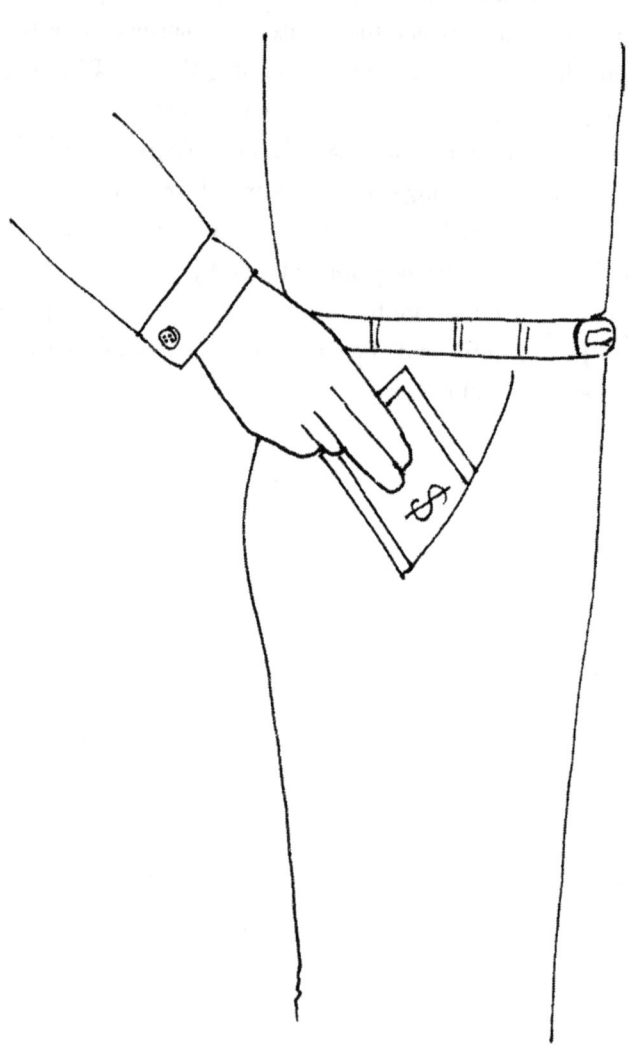

The cost related with travel on behalf of the company must be budgeted so that nothing is spent by the salesperson from his personal account.

Bhatta or daily allowance is the most common term used in all situations where sales personnel travel to the market either in the local city or in cities away from the base location.

The underlying principle of a daily allowance is to ensure that the salesperson does not go out of pocket to take care of his own expenses when he travels to the market either local or outstation. He is not expected to spend from his salary for anything when on travel or when he visits the market. This principle is adopted to ensure that the salesperson would plan his visit to the market without the apprehension that such a visit will result in him incurring additional expense. If this assurance is available to the salesperson, then visits to the market would be planned based on market needs and not get influenced by the fear of incurring extra expense.

As mentioned earlier, the job of the salesperson comprises days spent in the market and days spent in the office.

When the salesperson attends office, he has his routine expenses such as expense incurred on travelling back and forth to office, food expense, communication expense and other personal expenses, all of which he spends out of his salary.

When the salesperson goes to the market, there is a cost incurred beyond his normal personal expenses. For instance, when he travels to the market in the base city, he has to spend on food when in the market and may not be able to have his lunch from his routine source. This is an extra expense incurred only due to travel to market. So, this and other similar extra expense needs to be compensated by the company when on market visit in the base city.

Similarly, when the employee is expected to travel out of town involving night halts away from home, other expenses will be incurred which otherwise would have been taken care of when staying in the base city. For instance, expenses towards local travel, hotel stay, food, laundry, communication and several other miscellaneous expenses would incur for the entire period he is away from the base city. This needs to be taken care of by the company and cannot be expected to be met out of the salary of the salesperson. Some companies club hotel cost as part of daily allowance and others charge for it separately based on pre-specified budgets assigned to each city.

For administrative ease, most companies give a consolidated allowance to cover such extra expense incurred during the market visits in the base city or in locations outside the base city. They are often categorized as local travel allowance and outstation travel allowance.

Over and above the items of expense listed is the travel cost from city to city. So, cost of travel by the approved mode of travel should be compensated thereby ensuring that salespersons do not go out of pocket due to visits to market in either the base city or in locations outside the base city. Some companies arrange for purchase of tickets based on approved travel, other companies expect the salesperson to purchase their own tickets as per approved travel mode and get the cost reimbursed from the company.

When the company arrives at a budget cost of such allowances to be paid for travel to market, it keeps in mind the standards of travel and stay expected to be maintained by company personnel. For instance, companies expect their employees to travel in comfort by AC 1st or 2nd class, or by luxury AC bus or for distant markets by air. Similarly, they expect their employees to stay at clean and safe hotels. It will become necessary to ensure that the sales personnel use the prescribed modes of travel and hotel stay and actually incur the estimated expense and avoid falling into the temptation of using lower cost options for travel and stay to enable them to save for themselves some money. This is surely not to be encouraged as it has implications on safety and security of employees besides a compromise on values expected to be adhered to by the employees.

33

What Is the Role of Salary and Incentives?

There is a fine balance to be maintained between salary and variable pay. There are both positives and negatives that come into play if this is not properly planned.

We all work to earn an income that would support our needs and desires in the best way possible.

Income can be broadly divided into two categories—fixed income and variable income which is otherwise known as incentive. Both can be used to support the needs and desires of the employee.

What are the characteristics of these two categories of income?

Fixed Income

This income is assured to the employee in return for performing the role for which he has been hired by the company. It does not vary from month to month. It is earned as long as the individual is an employee of the company. This income, which is fixed, is known as salary and is received every month within a specified date.

Since the amount is fixed, and will be received as long as the individual is an employee of the company, he can plan his expenses accordingly. Does it change over a period of time? Yes, it does increase when there is an upgradation of the employee to roles which have higher level of responsibilities either operational or managerial or both. It could also increase over a period of time based on the standard increment given every year to compensate for the inflation levels experienced in the country. In sum, the employee sees this as an assured income based on which the employee plans his life.

Variable Income

This income is not assured to the employee every month or every year. It is earned by the employee only if he achieves the agreed-upon monthly/quarterly/yearly targets. So in order to earn incentives, employee would require to ensure that he meets/exceeds his targets.

Such targets could be volume targets, sales turnover targets, profitability targets or any other similar performance metrics that a salesperson is expected to do his best to achieve in a given period of time.

Income earned based on achievement of targets is known as variable income or incentive. Neither the amount earned is assured nor is the time of earning assured. As such income is not fixed in terms of time or amount, employees cannot plan to support routine expense from this category of income.

Organizations would also need to take into consideration the taxation laws prevailing in the country so that they ensure that the total earnings of the employee is liable to the least taxation level. In other words, maximize post-tax earnings of the employee. This surely does not mean avoiding payment of tax. It only means that the company takes interest in minimizing the tax liability of the employees while complying with the tax laws of the land.

Organizations also consider incentives that do not involve cash payouts but offer options such as holidays abroad, gift vouchers for dining at luxury hotels, even routine gifts for the employees and their families and many more innovative options to make the incentive attractive.

Different employees respond to the above two categories of income—fixed and variable—in different ways as much as they would respond to any situation. Such differences arise from the basic differences in people on how they handle their lives.

People Placing High Priority on Fixed Income

Some people are comfortable with a sense of security and hence give high weightage to options that provide the desired level of assured income stream every month. They feel they can plan their lives in an organized manner based on the assurance that they will receive the fixed monthly salary committed by the company. They do not want anxiety or uncertainty in receipt of such income and hence are far more comfortable when assured income is received at predetermined dates, which helps them plan their expense accordingly.

These types of people aim for growth in income through upgradation of their roles that may be awarded due to their good performance over a period of time in the company.

People Placing High Priority on Variable Income

There are others who get higher levels of satisfaction, if, over and above the fixed monthly income, they earn a significant amount on a monthly, quarterly or even annual basis as incentive for achieving a given level of performance.

They get motivated by the sheer opportunity to earn high variable income and work extra hard to make sure that they earn that additional money in the form of incentive and use it for expenses or savings which are not possible to be supported by the fixed income received from the company.

Sales personnel in most of the cases fall into the second category of people who get high satisfaction in working towards earning incentives based on achieving agreed-upon performance levels.

The question to be answered by business owners is what should be the percentage of total earning of employees that is to be assigned to the fixed-income category and what should be the percentage assigned to the variable-income (incentive) category.

Factors Influencing Such Decisions

* Degree of initiative expected from the sales personnel to achieve the desired targets.

- Extent of competitive presence in the industry which requires considerable pro-active steps by the individual sales personnel.
- Extent of gain in market share expected to be achieved in a given period.
- Risk profile of employees, often influenced by age profile.
- Marginal costing of product or service that determines the extent of incentive that could be supported for incremental sales.
- Life cycle of the products being sold. Products in the market at the introduction stage would require far more initiative from the sales personnel in comparison to products in the maturity stage of their life cycle.
- Salary practices in the industry or comparable industries.

Based on the above, decisions could be taken to determine the share of fixed and variable incomes in the total income budgeted for the employee. According to this decision, the various incentive schemes could be designed to offer the employee an opportunity to earn the maximum possible incentive during the course of the year.

Section IX

Ways to Encourage People to Buy More or Sell More

The system of selling is designed for a specific product to generate routine sales at all levels of the distribution chain, right up to the final consumer. However, to achieve sales volumes higher than the norm during a short period of time, one needs to consider offering incentive to the buyer to buy more than the normal level.

34

What Is Sales Promotion and When Is It Required?

BREAKFAST
CEREAL

FREE
GIFT
INSIDE

Sales promotion is a very common term used in the field of sales, as anyone involved in sales is always keen to sell more than normal. The question is what is more than normal and in what period of time is one expecting to achieve the same.

A given selling system is designed to achieve a desired volume of sales periodically, be it daily, weekly, monthly or annually. This sale could be at any level of the distribution chain—from the company to the distributors or from distributors to wholesalers or from distributors/wholesalers to retailers or even from retailers to final consumers.

When the selling system achieves the desired volume of sales, the intermediaries involved in the selling system earn the expected level of income based on the agreed-upon margins provided in the pricing of the product. So, the distributor, wholesaler or the retailer earn their expected income on achieving the desired level of sales volume.

But the reality in the market is far from comfort of such certainty. The uncertainty of various factors leading to less than the desired sales volume could be caused by unanticipated competitive pressure or demand drops within the industry or across industry or could even be due to unexpected seasonal factors, none of which we have control over.

In order to overcome the effect of the downward swings in sales volume caused by these unanticipated factors, sales teams often design a sales promotion to make good the loss in sales volume. While such sales promotions are run in response to market trends that have happened, there are other sales promotions that are run in anticipation of certain events such as high purchase season, festival season, holiday season and so on.

Sales promotion targeted at the various intermediaries in the distribution chain results in customers buying more than quantity that they would normally buy, ending up in higher than normal inventory levels stored. A distributor with average purchase volume of 1,000 units per month may decide to buy 1,100 when the company operates a sales promotion scheme. The distributor would have bought this additional 10 per cent quantity only because he has earned the additional benefit of sales promotion scheme operated by the company.

Having bought the higher quantity, he would be expected to invest additional time and resources to increase his sales volumes for the period ahead such that his extra inventory gets liquidated. Additional resources being spent by distributor in the market would be supported by the additional margins earned due to sales promotion conducted by the company.

The above process is applicable for any reseller, be it a distributor, a wholesaler or a retailer. Sales promotion, when targeted at the reseller, is often called *trade promotion schemes*.

Sales promotion, when targeted at the end consumer, is known as *consumer promotion schemes*. Such schemes are operated with the sole objective of increasing sales to consumer in a given timeframe. Higher sales at consumer level can be achieved in any of the following situations:

- Consumers are provided incentive to buy the product within a specific period, which induces them to advance their purchases which otherwise would have been bought at a later point in time.
- Consumers are provided incentive to buy higher volume of product compared to the normal volumes bought when the company does not operate a consumer promotion scheme.
- Consumers are provided incentives to switch away from their normal brand and buy this brand which offers a consumer promotion scheme.

The above are a few typical scenarios that trigger higher sales volumes.

35

What Are the Types of Sales Promotions Normally Seen?

The market invariably offers significant opportunities to operate sales promotion scheme at both the trade level and the consumer level.

The wide variety of schemes operated in the market for products in various industries could be classified into a few broad categories for ease of understanding.

Special discount for purchase of higher volumes within a specified period

- This scheme, when offered to trade partners, means higher margin for their business. Hence, trade partners would require to make a decision to buy higher volumes based on their own ability to sell. This judgement would also determine the method they propose to adopt to sell higher volumes to their customers and whether they would benefit from this transaction of higher volumes in the given period.

- For instance, if a 10 per cent special discount is being offered for all purchases made in the current quarter, the trade partner would need to make an assessment on how much he would be able to sell in the same quarter if he decides to pass on a share of the special discount of 10 per cent earned from the company. What would be the sales if he offers to his customers a discount of 5 per cent, 8 per cent or even 10 per cent are the various scenarios he would need to evaluate before he decides to buy the additional volume during the special discount offer by the company.

Such schemes are offered at both the trade level and at the consumer level as special discounts trigger higher sale in both. The only difference in consumer-level decision making is that the consumer evaluates the special discount offer based on how useful it is for him or her to buy the additional quantity.

Buy two get one free

- This is just another way of offering special discounts. The attractiveness of this approach to offer free product is based on COG compared to sales value, packaging issues, tax implications and acceptability of such offers in the industry and many such industry specific factors.
- This scheme can also be offered at both the trade level and consumer level. Once again, the consumer evaluates the offer based on how useful it is for him or her to buy the additional quantity.

Buy one product and get another product free

- This is often used to sell one product based on the attractiveness of another product. If product B is a high-selling product and product A is a product that is not in such high demand, then offering a given quantity of B free on the sale of a given quantity of A makes the sale offer of product A more attractive than the normal situation and thus get higher sales volume of product A.
- Sometimes companies use this method to test the market for a new product. If product Y is in the test-market phase and the company wants to get a preliminary feedback on product Y, it is offered free along with sales of product X, especially when the market for products X and Y are similar. Use of this option exposes product Y to the market or customers of product X and thus offers opportunity to the company to obtain market feedback on product Y.

Incentive for loyalty

- Marketeers of products that are bought frequently often find the need to ensure that customers purchase their products regularly. For monthly purchase items, marketeers are keen to ensure that every customer of theirs buy their products every month and do not switch over to other brands even on trial basis.

- In order to address this need, sales promotion campaigns are designed in a manner that customers earn a benefit if they show evidence of regular purchase. For example, some schemes involve submission of a given number of labels of the product over a period of time which entitles the customer to some benefit. Such benefits could be offered in the form of discount for future purchase or additional free product, etc.

- Airlines industry and hotel industry offer such incentive for regular use of their airlines or hotels. In the airline industry, these are called frequent flyer mileage points that can be re-deemed for a range of customer benefits. The hotel industry also offers additional benefits for customers who frequently stay at their hotel. Such offers could be in the form of premium cards that entitles the holder to a range of benefits at the hotel or even other services or products beyond those offered by the hotel.

Although there are a large variety of sales promotions schemes that are offered in the marketplace only few of them are very successful. So, it's extremely important to understand customer needs and buying habits to design an effective sales promotion scheme for a given product to ensure success.

36

Do Sales Promotion Schemes Get Misused?

When designing a sales promotion scheme, one does take into consideration all the guidelines that may be necessary to make it effective. But the ground reality in the implementation of these guidelines may not be as expected.

Sales promotion schemes are designed based on the assumption that those involved in the scheme implement the same as per guidelines communicated. The designers of the scheme therefore build in adequate checks and balances that would reduce, if not eliminate, deviations from the guideline.

However, the ground reality is that schemes are often misused, which results in unintended consequences of offering sales promotion schemes.

It is therefore useful to be aware of a few possible ways in which schemes are misused so that adequate safety measures are built into the design of the scheme.

Special discount for purchase of higher volumes within a specified period

- The buyer purchases higher quantity in the specified period and earns the special discount but does not use the additional discount to get higher sales and instead simply increases his own margin. Buyers usually buy less in the following period to liquidate high inventories resulting from his previous higher purchase under the special discount scheme.

- The company therefore does not achieve the objective of implementing the sales promotion scheme to increase sales.

Buy two get one free

- The buyer gets the free product on his purchases but does not offer the free on his sale and as a result does not increase sales in his area. This too ends with the company not achieving the objective of implementing the sales promotion scheme to increase sales.

- Such misuse however is not possible in the case of sales promotion scheme operated at the consumer level, if care is taken to print the details of the scheme on the product packaging or scheme details widely advertised in the media.

Incentive for loyalty

- As the scheme is offered based on the record of previous purchases, there is a danger of misreporting the previous purchases in order to gain the benefit of the scheme. This could be at the trade level or even at the consumer level. So, the sales promotion scheme budget gets misused in the market in the absence of reliable data of past purchases.

Other ways in which schemes can be misused

- Another weak spot liable to be misused is observed in schemes that specify minimum volume for being eligible to get the special discount. In such a scheme, invariably the financially strong trade partners buy quantity that is far more than what their own market requires, just in order to qualify for the special discount. Having earned the special discount, distributors then discount the product in the wholesale market to liquidate the extra quantity they bought under the scheme. Such a step by big distributors prevent smaller distributors from selling their inventory at their normal price simply because of stock inflow from outside wholesalers who have bought stock at a discount from the large distributors. In sum, it upsets the wholesale price in the market.
- Risk of collusion between salesperson and the distributor is another important concern area. Schemes are misused by the

distributors, and the same is overlooked by the salesperson simply because he is under pressure to achieve his sales targets for the period of the scheme.

All the above possibilities are related to one's own sales promotion scheme being misused and resulting in the objective being not achieved.

There are other scenarios as well that result in the scheme not achieving the desired objective. This happens when competition neutralizes the effect of your scheme by announcing their scheme which may be equal or better than the scheme which you have implemented in the market. This quick response from competition completely derails the entire sales promotion scheme as your products lose the desired competitive edge which would have been there had competition not implemented their scheme.

37

Do We Need to Evaluate the Effectiveness of Sales Promotion?

Whenever there is a decision to spend money to get a benefit, there is a need for a structured approach from the designing stage to the implementation stage. An evaluation of the entire process from planning to implementation, including results achieved, would be a very useful reference document for the future.

Sales is an ongoing process; it never stops unless consumers decide one fine day to stop buying your product or service. The selling system is therefore expected to handle such a continuous process day after day, month after month and year after year.

The experience gained over the years enables you to identify the need for a sales promotion scheme for a given range of products in a given period of time to achieve the desired sales volume.

Therefore, when a sales promotion scheme is being designed in a professional manner, there is a recommended template for the designer to consider all important parameters and introduce checks and balances to make the scheme effective in the marketplace.

The key elements of the template are listed below for ready reference.

Designing stage:

- Product category/product type
- Sales overview of the identified product, for the preceding years
- Sales overview of the identified product, for the recent period
- Sales volumes anticipated in a scenario without sales promotion
- Sales volumes anticipated in a scenario with sales promotion
- Sales overview related to competitive scenario
- Justification for additional input in the form of sales promotion scheme
- Target market for the implementation of sales promotion scheme

- Scheme details
- Scheme period
- Cost of scheme
- Communication of scheme details to the field, mode and timing
- Concern areas identified in the implementation of scheme
- Anticipated response from competition
- Desired results in the specific period

Review stage:

- Review of implementation of scheme, mid scheme and post scheme
- Review of results of scheme, after the end of the scheme period

The list of elements in the template indicates the need for a structured approach right from the Design stage. This commences with an evaluation of the need for a scheme including a rationale for running it. It will also specify the cost and time parameters besides the sales volumes to be achieved.

Sales team often use sales promotion as an insurance against dips in volumes. As the sales teams are rarely accountable for profits, the cost for the implementation of sales promotion schemes does not find a place in the consideration list. It is for the management team to evaluate the demand for a sales promotion scheme and hence the need for a structured template that helps the designer to put down his understanding of the market scenario and then evaluate the need for a sales promotion scheme.

Sometimes, after the exercise of evaluating the need for a sales promotion scheme, a situation may emerge that may not find justification for a sales promotion scheme, hence requiring a rejection of demand for such inputs to increase sales.

The review stage on the other hand focuses on mid-scheme review and end-of-scheme review.

The purpose of mid-scheme review is to take stock as per the scheme across markets where it has been implemented and to see whether there have been any surprises requiring mid-course corrective steps. This review would also include the effectiveness of the communication of the scheme details, the compliance to guidelines by field personnel and the availability of the planned resources for implementation in the market. This review should also have a quick overview of the response from competition to such a scheme and the possible impact on results if there is a competitive response. At the end of this mid-course review, there is a need to identify areas where corrective action is to be initiated, if any.

The post-scheme review provides a structured evaluation of every element listed in the scheme design stage and the review of each stage ending with an observation whether the scheme was implemented as per the plan and whether the results achieved were as per the plan. If the implementation of the scheme was not as per the plan, then there is a need to evaluate the causative factors for such shortfall, followed by a recommendation of steps to be taken in future to ensure that such deviations do not recur.

A similar process is followed to evaluate the results of the sales promotion scheme to understand the cause of deviation if any and also identify steps to be taken in future to ensure that such deviations do not recur.

Such a system of evaluation of all sales promotion schemes helps build a reservoir of knowledge in the management team that helps in deciding the future sales promotion schemes as and when considered.

Section X

Keeping the Spark Alive

A fully engaged sales team produces much better results than one that is listless. There are many ways to ensure that the sales team is finely tuned.

38

The Dangers of Sales Team Losing Interest in Their Job

Startups are chronic for sales mostly fall short of targets. Salespeople often take the blame for this happening and do not see a light at the end of the tunnel. Looking for another job is an easy solution. This further complicates the selling process.

It is said that manning a startup is difficult. Few, if any, want to commit themselves to an unknown entity. Most of the job candidates worry about how successful they can be. Joining an established company itself poses its share of troubles. Add to it the uncertainty of a new industry, new company and a new career. A cocktail designed in hell.

No Awareness

The launch of a new product is accompanied by a frenzy of publicity. This however is short-lived as sustaining the same level of activity is just not affordable. Before long, the last vestiges of the launch evaporate and no one hears about the fabulous new launch, the products placed so proudly are up for returns. When a product is returned for poor off-take, it is the kiss-of-death as far as the product launch goes.

When this happens, the poor salesperson has a nearly unsurmountable task of facing the market, with a drooping confidence and a fast disappearing order pipeline. This is accompanied by a litany of insults and taunts from the sales bosses, who imagine that threatening their livelihood will magically inject life into the dying brand. Faced with these dire consequences, the way out seems suicidal, but attractive.

Be in the Trenches

Sales management for startups has to be close to the action. The mere fact that a product has reached the stage that it could be returned shows an unhealthy distance from the users. Traditionally, there are three stages of monitoring an off-take.

THE STARTUP'S GUIDE TO SALES

The first and most comforting to the revenue-starved startup is the 'primary sales'. This is the first level sales, that is, typically the invoicing from the factory gate or the company depot to the distributors. Tracking this as the health of the product can result in a severe jolt. The second level of sales, named, not surprisingly enough, as 'secondary sales', charts the sale from the distributor to the retailer, who will be the person to handle the final consumer. This, while an improved measure over the tracking of 'primary sales', is still not a real-time indicator of the health of the product.

The most efficient way is, of course, the tracking of sales from the retailer to the consumer—the 'tertiary sales'. Assuming that the consumer buys to use the product, and not store it, this is the real bloodline indicating the fate of the startup. Unfortunately, the champagne bottles are popped as the primary sales happen.

Count Activity, Not Sales

'The road is lonely dark and deep', as the poet Robert Frost predicted, and the effort at the launch of the startup has to be not on counting sales as much as to counting the achievements in an activity. The activities are the action steps that will lead on to meeting the goals. These are as important, if not more important, the sales numbers at the early stage of the startup.

Keep Morale High

A good sense of humour and the ability to appreciate the absurd is very useful. Leadership demand at this part of the life cycle is to have a sense of wonderment. Good news or bad, it still is exciting to have a startup. When your sales team sees that you are able to take the knocks without flinching, they will stay the course with you and not quit.

39

Need for the Spark to Keep Them Motivated and Perform at Their Peak

Sales leadership makes all the difference at this juncture. Performance of sales activities are necessary regardless of how poor the sales results are. This is not given the due importance.

Sales leadership is the call of the moment. The parallel with the army is not at all out of place. There are tales of valour that come from the battlefield of how the besieged platoon, bloodied and outnumbered still stood and fought like tigers. The battles of the sales arena are not as glorified, nor comparable, but provide a framework for how morale is kept high even when the odds appear indomitable. Some of the principles of comradeship are applicable.

Principle of Team

All for one and one for all, as such, seems a hash of corn. Yet, there is a sense of doing it for the team and, of not letting the team down, evokes a strong 'circle of morale' when the chips are down. There is an invaluable Persian adage, promoted by Og Mandino, the sales mystic, that simply says, 'This too shall pass'. This is the well of hope. Joy or sadness is fleeting, and, in moments of deep despair, this is the flotsam that one clings to. To float to safety.

Sales Leadership

Taking the cue from leadership in the battlefield, the sales head has a role that is invaluable to the power of the sales team. This role is often mistaken for the 'super salesperson'. The work of the frontline salesperson is clear and there is no ambiguity. The results show easily. However, the sales manager to whom the frontline report is often confusing.

When the orders fall short, the sales manager arrives on the scene. As the junior fails, there is a sense of intervention. Something similar to when the instructor-pilot allows the trainee to take the controls. When he finds the trainee is jeopardizing the flight, he takes over and lands the plane.

Intervention

This act of intervening is not a learning exercise but one of handing over controls. The sales manager has to worry not merely how to save the sales order for the month but also how to coach the salesperson to be able to do the sales independently.

At times, it might be the right decision to lose a sale but develop the team member. Unfortunately, there is too much of intervention in the guise of saving the sale for the month.

When the boss decides to step in and take charge, there is a show of authority to the customer and undue pressure put to make the sales order happen. The fresher salesperson has no experience nor the hierarchy to repeat what the boss does.

Develop the Team

The sole purpose of having a sales manager is to ensure that each of the team members has the competency to achieve the targets with no intervention from the boss. This cannot be achieved at month end; it has to be planned and worked upon with a clear-cut purpose.

The sales manager has to understand the competence level of each member of the sales team. According to the development of each person, inputs must be designed and implemented.

The sales manager must understand that the contribution expected by the company is not when an intervention takes place, but when coaching and guidance help move the salesperson to acquire a high degree of performance, without seeking support of the boss.

This is a unique contribution that only the sales manager can provide, as there is no one in the organization who steps in to develop a sales manager's junior. Sales managers must take pride of a self-driven and independent sales team.

40

Techniques to Keep the Sales Team Charged Up

Contrary to common wisdom, sales teams perform best when they are successful. Sales contests, trips abroad, cruise holidays and such other efforts to create interest, they are not guaranteed to help a startup succeed. Building positive relationships and developing people are the need of the hour.

Every sales manager does develop a unique style over the years. There are yet certain corner stones of sales management that have stood the test of time and have the propensity to be valid for the foreseeable future. Any novice in the profession of a sales manager could well incorporate the following values and not regret it.

Trust Them

To trust is hard to do when salespeople have a chequered reputation for transparency. Yet this is a two-way street. Trust begets trust. The sales manager who trusts the team in turn hopes that the team would trust him too. This is also a factor of how much risk-taking one is comfortable with.

Undoubtedly, there are numerous occasions where the trust is broken. In a single person's life, there can only be a few instances of this happening. The rest of the time, trusting without suspicion provides for many occasions of satisfaction. The quality of the fellowship is hard to define when trust is the foundation. The difference is easily felt.

Trust is the basis of all relationships. In a team, it becomes the binding factor. To go back to the army example, the level of trust is so high that in a war situation, each person trusts their lives with the team members. Relationships without trust are mere transactions and there is no depth.

Communication Beyond Need to Know

There is a stern admonishment in management circles. 'Team members have to be communicated on a principle of "need to know" only.' Excessive information could cause much confusion and some possible loss.

This, although well intentioned, considers every individual as a cog in a giant machine. This attitude does limit commitment. Treating an individual as a thinking being does require giving more information than just need to know.

Mature adults can identify with an action if they are given to understand why it is important and needed in reaching the goals set by the organization.

Recently, in the example of Jet Airways that went bankrupt, the airline had to gradually drop a number of facilities like lounge access to their frequent flyer members. Instead of just informing the members as a routine, they shared the difficulties they were facing financially that caused the action to be taken. It helped get a more sympathetic response.

Teach Them Well

The act of teaching is a selfless one. Many hold their kindergarten teachers precious as they had a sense of gratitude for someone who shared their knowledge with so much concern. Sales managers too must take on the role of knowledge providers. Holding back information or skills will be known and considered an act of pure selfishness.

At times, there is an unspoken rivalry where the boss fears that the team member could actually overtake the instructor. Perhaps also exceed in sales what the master could produce. A teacher can take two approaches. The first one is of competing with the pupil. The other is to feel accomplished when the pupil exceeds the master in talent and performance.

Correct Them

If there is an uncalled for abuse of the limitations of the association, there must be no reluctance in calling out unacceptable behaviour.

There are genteel ways of putting across the reservation, without hurting anyone's feelings. One effective method is the 'itemized response' method which identifies the items done well while also not mincing the importance of improving the efforts.

Section XI

Sales Leadership

Hiring the best sales team is a part of the sales challenge. Leading the team to success is the real task. The nature of sales leadership is vital to their growth and development of the sales team members. This is a requisite for long-term growth of the startup.

41

How Is the Role of a Sales Manager Different from a Frontline Sales Personnel?

The sales manager is responsible for sales strategy and ensuring that it is implemented. The sales team is responsible for getting things done. Each member must be competent to complete all functions of the job without the help of the sales manager. Developing the people to be independent is the single most important contribution of the sales manager.

In a small startup unit, there may not be a large enough sales team. Even a two-man sales team needs a sales manager. If there is no sales manager, then the head of the startup has to step in and do the job. So, what really are the roles in this function?

Goal Setting

The startup has dreams that need to come true. These visions of paradise need to have clear-cut goals, or targets, that need to be met. These have to be quantifiable and tangible, not fuzzy. Most of all, there is a need to agree on a mutually respected deadline.

Strategy

The sales goal will only be achieved when the strategy has a possibility of winning the day. The action of strategy building falls squarely on the sales manager. With a simple strategy in place, the sales manager has to learn to appreciate. The easier way to achieve goals is to have a reasonable game plan and stick to it. This is the task of the sales manager.

Action Plans

Even after setting a tangible, measurable goal and a reasonable strategy, it is still miles away before anything substantial can be achieved. This is only done when a detailed step-by-step documentation of the implementation methods are recorded and completed.

It is important that these action steps be as realistic and chronological as possible. They must be dated. Each step must have a deadline and the salesperson must be obliged to meet or complete the action step in time.

Often, the steps as planned may not fructify on the day planned. When this happens, a revised plan must be indicated so that the schedule for the subsequent action plans is not disturbed.

Risk

The best laid-out plans sometimes don't get started. This does happen and this information is held back from management. Consider the goal is to launch a new sales promotion to sell more volumes. The strategy and action steps are put into place but the salesperson does not implement. Yet, when asked by the management, instead of informing that the strategy is not implemented, a vague report is sent saying the new sales promotion is slowly taking root. Without an accurate first information report, the production continues at enhanced levels.

When finally the scheme is implemented in the field, it is realized that the increase in sales is not possible. Now the management is informed hastily. By which time the production has already completed the goals set. It is now too late to make changes in strategy, and there is a loss to the company. On top of that, it is required to review everything and to set a new plan in motion.

The sales team is the critical part of the success in any sales strategy. Unless they are skilled at quick implementation, any major thrust in the field will fall short. If the team is poorly trained to implement plans, there is a risk that a good plan and excellent strategy may be dropped without realizing that the fault lay not with the strategy but with the implementation.

It is quite possible that in an attempt to remedy the situation, a new plan and another brand-new strategy is put in place, when all that was needed was better implementation of the original plan.

It is the sales manager who needs to ensure that implementation is completed professionally.

42

How to Make the Sales Manager Lead the Team Effectively?

Incompetent sales managers raise the decibel of their voice to substitute for declining sales. A startup may have months when their targets are not met. It is the role of the sales manager to assess where the team members fall short and be ready to coach them for greater success.

Sales teams that have a startup challenge need to be selected for their capability to deal with ambiguity and lack of system. The initial months are chaotic, and, unless a special effort is taken to bring things under control, the mayhem can maim the startup seriously.

Plan Going Wrong

There was a startup that had made sure that they staffed the positions with veterans of the industry. It was expected to be smooth sailing. Hardly a month went by when there were many cries for help. The company was in crisis mode.

Many of the staff members refused to speak to each other. Quality went crashing down. The decibel levels were rising dangerously. People were shouting at each other, simultaneously. Paradise seemed lost. Until an action was taken.

Introspection

A behavioural expert was called to help alleviate the situation. A number of 'let's be open sessions' were held and a number of resolutions were taken to reduce the toxicity of the interpersonal relations. Such introspection did lead to some favourable results and, in the space of three months, frayed tempers were patched up and results started to show.

A new company has poor systems and work allocation is done on an ad-hoc, must-be-finished basis. The sales set-up is no different. Many a sales call is a cold one and the salesperson is firing in the dark. So, what is the most effective manner of leading the sales team?

THE STARTUP'S GUIDE TO SALES

According to Need

The time spent with the salesperson has to be a factor of the maturity stage of the new recruit. Rawer the salesperson, more of the sales manager's time is to be allocated to the OJT of the employee.

Classroom training has its limitation. There is a need for rigorous coaching. It is through a systematic kerbside counselling and demos that a skill is embedded.

Discipline to Motivate

There are times when, in the issues of discipline, there is social pressure to soft-pedal and to avoid taking a stand. There are accusations of not being in tune with the times. Even to the extent of, possibly, being impractical.

Amit was a salesperson beyond the cut. He always had the order, even as others would struggle. Especially in poor sales months, he could be counted on to deliver, regardless. Amit had an extravagant style and there was idle gossip in the dressing room about how could he afford the luxury brands he used on a salesperson's salary. Until, internal audit swooped on his expense reports.

Amit had a number of irons in the fire. He had tampered with his food bills. Even more, he had booked first-class train travel, and, before the day of travel, cancelled the ticket and taken a bus instead. He would present the ticket booked online for the premium train travel. Amit's defence was self-righteous.

The bills were not exceeding what the company allowance was for travel. He had opted to travel by bus, at great personal discomfort, even though the company allowed him first-class travel. There was no loss to the company. Every expense was within the budget. HR asked that Amit be terminated for lack of integrity. Amit's sales manager, Rohit, was really upset. He was not going to lose his main batsman.

Rohit argued that standards of morality were no longer cast in stone. There is open cheating in board exams, corruption rife in all levels of life. He also dropped a bomb: 'If he is sacked, I will not be able to meet targets.'

Faced with the woes of being a startup, what would be your decision?

Integrity at What Cost?

A sales team is a street savvy one. With no one stating it, they catch on easily to the values that guide the campaign. They do in fact search for clues that tell what the dispensation is for discipline. Sales teams that lag in discipline are poor in cohesiveness.

The moment a salesperson senses that there is an air of lax control, the individual objectives start edging out the company goals and soon there is a real problem. Being gentle and kind is in no way an indication of the sales manager being poor on control. Not taking action on those who break rules is a statement, even if no words are spoken.

A sales team needs to believe in the nobility of their purpose. The greatest performances happen not just with pure talent. Mix a sense of purpose with any level of talent and you can get spectacular results. Any visit to an army cantonment will amaze, as how much is invested in getting the troops to believe in a world of values that may exist only in one's mind. Discipline and integrity are never sacrificed at the altar of expediency.

In the bottom line, integrity is priceless and profitable.

43

Simple Techniques to Keep the Team Performing at Peak Levels

Feedback and guidance on a continuous basis are the keys to improving performance. Failure to perform to a given target must not be considered a deficiency of the salesperson as much as the need to improve the sales process.

Sales performance is often difficult to understand. Is it a personal skill or a relevant sales process? The super salespersons in a sales team give the profession a touch of magic. They are personable, say the most appropriate things and literally charm the wallet off the willing and grateful customer.

Everyone is in awe of these special beings. Many try to copy aspects of such role models. In the old days, if a super salesperson walked with a swagger, the walk would be imitated. If chewing gum was a notable feature, many in the sales team would start chewing gum. However, mimicking traits don't make for a sales master. It further defines how futile the quest is to be a sales Zen master. It is nearly not possible to train and achieve this exalted sales status.

However, everyone in the sales team can be a professional salesperson.

To be a professional salesperson requires a broad mastery of sales skills and an adherence to a solid selling process.

Sales Skills: Learnable

The majority of the sales team does not fall into the sales maestro category. Instead of copying a swagger or an accent, there is a need to equip each salesperson on the basic selling skills.

These are not so much sales skills as they are life skills. Mastering these skills is easy for most, if they have an attitude for learning. Let's look at what these skills are.

Focus on Customer's Success

A professional salesperson has to understand that, at all times, the object of every effort is to seek the success of the customer. Most salespeople put their own success as a priority. No salesperson can be winning if the customer is losing. The customer is not to be seen as an opponent but a purpose of the salesperson's being. This is hard to accept, as decades of sales bravado has been to target the customer as an obstacle to success.

A professional salesperson understands this and keeps it as a credo of selling.

Handle Objections

In every salesperson's workday, a few 'no' will fall. A customer refusing to buy or one who is upset and is irate is a part of the package. No one can solve every objection that a customer raises or undo the damages of poor service.

This is an important skill that must be acquired by each salesperson. There are various methods suggested by sales experts. The one that makes immense sense is when the salesperson detaches from the emotion of the event and concentrates on finding out more about the issue under contest and tries to view it sympathetically from the customer's operating reality.

Having done everything that is needed to fully appreciate the source of the objection and the scope of the fallout, it is an honest attempt to seek some resolution, if possible. If not, at least leave the customer feeling that the salesperson handled the issue professionally.

Identify Customer Need

Every salesperson must believe that the sale is dependent on discovering the needs of the customer and, more importantly, to ensure that the need is confirmed as being truly the most relevant.

This skill is acquired by a set of simple questions being asked. This is the skill of asking questions in a pre-ordained manner. This assumes that there is an ability to listen carefully, skill of active listening.

The Pitch

The other important skill is to be able to present the product or the solution in a manner that creates an impact leading to a sales order.

The skill here is not just speaking in a forthright manner, but more in a logical way so that the decision-making process of the consumer is aided.

With these few skills, the professional salesperson is a reality. Anyone with resolve and intent can be one.

Sales Process

With these skills to use, the salesperson has all the weapons that make for success in the field. Yet there is a need to define a sales process relevant to the particular industry.

This too is not difficult to master. The sales manager has the responsibility to lay out a tangible step-by-step method of how to meet the customer, greet, achieve a positive contact and identify needs before giving the sales solution. Done this way, even super salespersons will be more successful.

Then, every other salesperson will be a professional and more than equal to the task of bringing in sales performance that meet the startup's goals.

Section XII

A Tribute to Startups, Wherever

The act of being a startup requires a stubborn commitment of getting to the goals. The heroes are all among us, and their claim to fame crosses the urban divide. This section is to highlight the work of two of them. Both have gone through the pain but have not given up hope.

Epilogue

STARTUP CHAMP

Paracasa, Udaipur

Swastik and Priti Ranka are college sweethearts who got married and carried their partnership into the business arena. They were not born with a silver spoon, as both sets of parents were salaried. Swastik's father is a renowned veterinary doctor, who was a government employee and still practices.

Brought up in the beautiful city of Udaipur, they are proud of their city and hope to make it known for the enterprise that abounds there. The city is an attractive tourist spot and has great historical value. Right in the centre of town there is a statute of Chetak, the horse that Maharana Pratap rode to battle. Legend has it that the faithful horse saved Maharana's life at the cost of his own. Typical of the young in this city, it is the future that excites.

Working as a team, Priti and Swastik started a showroom called 'Shade 'N Shelter', specializing in kitchen-related products. They were dealers for Franke, the world's most important sink manufacturer. They also were distributors of kitchen chimneys from Faber. Soon their showroom became the showpiece of modular kitchens in Udaipur.

Swastik was determined to create a homegrown brand that would be internationally known. In 2014, he put in all his life's savings, and whatever he could borrow, to create his own brand 'Paracasa'. In a modern factory, he was able to manufacture world-class shutters and cabinets for the modular kitchen industry.

Swastik went thru all the trials written about in this book. At a very difficult moment, he decided to build his own sales force. He followed most of the tips given in this book. Today he is probably the largest startup in Udaipur and is already considering a greenfield project where he would have space over five times his current leased property.

Saviesa, Mumbai

Rajesh Ahuja, a B. Tech graduate in mechanical engineering from Pune University. He was immediately asked to report to an office where he had to do work he hated. He decided instead that he would work for himself. His father, the late Thakur T. Ahuja realized that his oldest son had a mind of his own. He invested ₹50,000 to make wire baskets that Rajesh made in a small workshop.

Rajesh was like a man possessed. He worked late nights and proved to the workers that he could be more productive using skills he learnt at the engineering college. Soon he was making wire stands for product merchandizing and, then on, he was making the steel accessories that went into the kitchen. He found the going tough. As his younger brother, Monesh, graduated from college, he joined Rajesh in growing their startup.

One day, he had a bright idea. He decided that to allow consumers to fully appreciate the accessories he had been selling for the kitchen, he opened a showroom in Borivali. He built a modern-looking kitchen and displayed the steel accessories in the kitchen.

Imagine his surprise when there were more enquiries for the modern-looking kitchen than his accessories. He was asked to make the kitchen. He sold his first kitchen and over the years became the most important kitchen brand in India—Sleek.

Sleek grew to a pan-India presence and was acquired by Asian Paints as they were growing into the home-improvement sector. The brothers decided that they would create yet another brand, and, in 2018, Saviesa was established.

Today they are in the throes of the new startup and have had to relearn skills to handle the new enterprise. They have had early success, but the path is long and the road uphill. It is only the spirit of the startup that keeps them going.

They have started a whole new sales team and are rapidly building it up.

Startup: A Salute

There are thousands like Swastik, Priti, Rajesh and Monesh. This is what developing an economy is all about. There is a hunger right across the country: Be your own boss is the battle cry. No doubt there will be casualties along the way. There will be successes too. They will inspire others. The age of the startup is here and it will not go away.

Go and prosper.

Annexures

Annexure I. Classification of Distributors Using 80/20 Principle

Distributors Ranked by 80/20 Principle	Distributor's Names in Descending Order of Sales Value	Annual Sales Value of Distributor (₹lakhs)	Share of Total Territory Sales Value (%)	Cumulative Share of Total Territory Sales Value (%)	80/20 Classification (MAJ/MIN)	Share of Total Territory Sales Value (%)
20%	IFG	90	21	21	Major	80
	RET	85	20	40	Major	
	POU	75	17	58	Major	
	ABC	65	15	73	Major	
	TYO	35	8	81	Major	
80%	IPO	11	3	83	Minor	20
	YOU	10	2	86	Minor	
	TRY	8	2	88	Minor	
	TUS	6	1	89	Minor	
	XBY	5	1	90	Minor	
	DUR	5	1	91	Minor	
	RTY	5	1	92	Minor	
	GHK	4	1	93	Minor	
	DFG	4	1	94	Minor	
	GHI	4	1	95	Minor	
	IJK	4	1	96	Minor	
	LMN	4	1	97	Minor	
	OPQ	4	1	98	Minor	
	RST	3	1	99	Minor	
	UVW	3	1	99	Minor	
	XYZ	3	1	–		
	Total	433	100%	100%		

Annexure 2. Daily Market Report

Daily Market Report 2019–2020						Hashtag	
Zone		Branch		Territory			JC No.:
Code	ZN-000	Code	BR-000	Code	T-000	Date	JC-00

Distributor Visit

Name of Distributor	Dist. Code	Order Confirmed	Order Negotiation	Product	Quantity	Value	RS/KG	Other Issues

Retail Point Visit

Name of Retail Point Visited	Dist. Code	Product	Quantity	Value	Product	Quantity	Value	Remarks

New Distributor Activity

Name of Prospective Distributor	Market	Next Meeting/Plan of Action	Business Potential (MT)	Remarks

Working Details

Time of Meeting First Customer	Time In	Daily Bhatta	Transport	Others	Others	Total Expense	Signed
Time of Leaving Last Customer	Time Out						

Note: This report is prepared by an SE forwarded to the superior at the end of every day. SE to retain a copy in tab folder, one folder for each JC.

Annexure 3. Frequency of Visit Report

Zone		Branch		Territory		Average Purchase per Month (2018–2019)			Grade		Dates of Visit to Distributor													Re-marks	Hashtag
Code	ZN-000	CODE	BR-000	CODE	T-000																				
						Distributor Name	Quantity	Value	RS/ KG	MAJ/ MIN	Al-Grade	JC-1	JC-2	JC-3	JC-4	JC-5	JC-6	JC-7	JC-8	JC-9	JC-10	JC-11	JC-12	JC-13	
Distributor Code																									

Note: This report is prepared and presented by SE at every JC meeting for current and all past JCs, presented to the branch manger to file these reports in a folder that is maintained SE wise.

Annexure 4. Distributor Visit Report

Section I

Distributor Visit Report 2019–2020							Hashtag	
Zone		Branch		Territory				JC No.:
Code	ZN-000	Code	BR-000	Code			T-000	JC-00
							Quantity	Value RS/KG

Name of distributor		Annual purchase 2018–2019	
Distributor code		Average purchase per JC 2018–2019	
MAJ/MIN		YTD JC – no purchase 2018–2019	
Grade		YTD JC – no purchase 2019–2020	

Sr. No.	Topics Discussed	Action Taken	Action to Be Taken	Remarks
1				

Check List on Topics

Pending claims		Transport		Taxation	
Pending payments		Packaging		Product quality	
Pending documents		Invoicing		Delivery lead time	

Retail Point Visit

	Retail Orders Booked from Market Today		
	Product	Quantity	Value
No. of retail points stocking ABC brand and/or competition			
No. of retail points stocking ABC brand			
No. of ABC brand stocking retail points visited			
No. of new retail points visited			

Section II

Order Confirmed Today

Product Name	Product Code	Quantity	Delivery Terms	Price	ETD	Remarks

Order Awaiting Confirmation

Product Name	Product Code	Quantity	Delivery Terms	Price	ETD	Remarks

Current Visit Record Details

Visit Date		Signature	
Plan Date as per JC		Signed By	
Actual Visit Date		Approved By	

Next Visit Schedule
Remarks

Visit Personnel

Self	
Self + superior	
Superior	
Others	

Note: This report is prepared by SE at the end of every distributor visit, using own inputs and inputs from DMR and other reports.

Annexure 5. Planned Journey Cycle

Section I

	Planned Journey Cycle						Hashtag
Zone		Branch		Territory			JC No:
Code	ZN-000	Code	BR-000	Code	T-000		JC-00
		MAJMIN		MAJMIN		MAJMIN	MAJMIN
Week	Date	Distributor Name	Distributor Name	Distributor Name	Distributor Name	Distributor Name	Distributor Name
1							
1							
1							
1							
1							
1							
2							
2							
2							
2							
2							
2							

JC Meeting Day

Section II

Week	Date	Distributor Name	MAJMIN	Distributor Name	MAJMIN	Distributor Name	MAJMIN	Distributor Name	MAJMIN	Distributor Name	MAJMIN
3											
3											
3											
3											
3											
4											
4											
4											
4											
4											
JC Meeting Day											

	Special Objective/Remarks		Signed By	Date
Employee name				
Designation				
Name of superior			Approved By	Date
Designation				

Note: This report is prepared by SE at the last meeting of preceding JC and approval of superior obtained.

About the Authors

Roshan L. Joseph is a professional in the sales and marketing field and a consultant of repute. He has been the Executive Director on the Board of Eveready Industries India Ltd with the accountability for marketing and sales. He has also been the Managing Director (MD) of Franke, a Swiss MNC in the kitchen solutions business. At Eveready, he was instrumental in bringing Eveready out of the cold with the pathbreaking advertising campaign 'Give Me Red'. This brought about the repositioning of Eveready as a brand that could connect with the youth. The campaign won 11 advertising and marketing awards and continues to date with the way Eveready advertises. Earlier on, his skills as a marketer were put to test in a challenge facing the flashlight business. This was the neglected business of the company. Today, with adept marketing moves, it is a very profitable division of the company.

In 2004, Roshan, as the MD of Franke, had the challenge of establishing the brand, though no. 1 worldwide, in the Indian kitchen scene. Today, Franke is well established as a premium brand of kitchen sinks. Here too, he established a unique positioning and improved distribution to develop the brand.

In 2007, he started a marketing and sales development company of his own in collaboration with Carew International of Cincinnati, USA. He has worked with diverse clients across the Middle East and India. Roshan has been a trainer as far back as he can remember. He has been the Course Director of the Calcutta Management Association for a record six years. He established the first Sales Training Department in the company. He was the Founder of the Eveready Academy of Sales Training (EAST) and was instrumental in the award-winning initiative Basic Training Program for training all employees of Union Carbide, over 6,000 of them.

Roshan is currently the Managing Partner of B-More Consulting (www.bmoreconsulting.net), where he promotes various international sales development initiatives.

Ram Mohan Menon (IIMA Class of '78) is a sales and marketing professional. A sales trainer of repute, he is also a management consultant. He has held various senior management positions at Eveready in the sales and marketing function. He retired from Eveready as the Executive Vice President.

His marketing experience covers a wide range of goods, including frozen marine products, batteries, flashlights and tea, both in domestic and international markets. He has played a major role in improving the efficiencies of the distribution system at Eveready. He spearheaded the establishment of a new brand of batteries for the export market which included various countries in Africa, Sri Lanka, Bangladesh and Nepal. This role saw him handling the challenges of sales and distribution in a global context.

As a consultant, he has been engaged in the assessment of the sales process and management system prevailing in client organizations and redesigning them for greater operational efficiency. These client organizations belonged to a wide range of industries such as footwear, pipe and fittings, chemical, electric two-wheeler industry and several others. As a trainer, he has conducted sales training programmes offered by Carew International, USA, for various organizations in India. He is also a visiting professor at a leading management college in Kolkata.

You can contact Roshan Louis Joseph and Ram Mohan Menon at roshanlouisjoseph@gmail.com and ramsworld1@gmail.com respectively.